# Past Lives, Dreams, and Soul Travel

# Also by Harold Klemp

# Past Lives, Dreams, *and* Soul Travel

Harold Klemp

ECKANKAR
Minneapolis
www.Eckankar.org

## Past Lives, Dreams, and Soul Travel

Printed in USA
ISBN: 978-1-57043-182-1
Compiled by Mary Carroll Moore
Edited by Joan Klemp and Anthony Moore
Text illustrations by Rebecca Lorio
Cover illustration by Merrill Peterson
Cover design by Doug Munson
Third printing—2013


Library of Congress Cataloging-in-Publication Data

Klemp, Harold.
    Past lives, dreams, and soul travel / Harold Klemp.
      p. cm.
    Includes index.
    ISBN 1-57043-182-5 (alk. paper)
      1. Eckankar (Organization) 2. Reincarnation. 3. Dreams. 4. Astral projection. I. Title.

    BP605.E3 K56465 2003
    299'.93—dc21

                                        2002029954


∞ This paper meets the requirements of ANSI/NISO Z39.48-1992 (Permanence of Paper).

# Contents

# Introduction

*A* certain belief was drummed into me as a boy about life after death. It was the idea that at death Soul "sleeps" until the final day of judgment, that death marks a time of complete unconsciousness. But this notion rang like a wooden sleigh bell.

To me, such a state of death afforded the horrors of a nightmare.

I grew up on a farm. Family life meant raising and caring for horses, cattle, hogs, chickens, cats, and a couple of dogs, as well as planting crops to feed them and us. But just as important, our family felt a pull toward our church on Sundays for spiritual food. Church was at once a religious and a social center. Of course, all came to worship God, but the day's spice was the after-worship visit with neighbors outside the church doors.

Men weighed in on land, cattle, crops, or local issues. Women scarfed up tidbits about family, health, cooking, or their kids at school. Boys kidded each other, while girls shared their own brand of concerns or silliness.

However, few discussed religion. The church service was over.

Nearly everyone in church was part of some bigger family circle. It was natural, then, that everyone knew everyone else, so a church service was a reunion of friends and relatives.

During those years, Grandpa and Grandma often lived on the family farm with one of their adult children. The grandparents, wise and beloved elders, helped care for the grandchildren, did light chores, but still rode herd on their grown children. In time, of course, the old ones would pass on one by one. The day of such a one's funeral was like a Sunday in that farmers did the bare morning and evening chores, milking cows and cleaning the barn.

A Soul's passing was thus a day of worship, yet one of sadness too.

Children were on hand the days or weeks before a grandparent's passing. The process of dying had not yet become sanitized and hidden away as it is today, when the sick and elderly go to age and die away from home. The fact of dying happened right before our eyes. We saw death on many occasions.

While death meant the loss of someone near and dear to us, it was not the mysterious vanishing of an elder seen but once or twice a year on some festive occasion.

More than that, a rural child watched parents and neighbors prepare for the funeral. He overheard them on the phone. They called each other to express sorrow, offer consolation, and perhaps give a gentle commentary about the good character of the departed—whether true or not.

The final good-byes came at church. Whole families, from baby to most feeble elder, attended the funeral service if health and weather allowed. Our congregation first listened to the pastor give the funeral blessings. Then, the entire assembly filed out to the cemetery by the church where the coffin's vault sank into a dark, gloomy hole and the piles of fresh earth were tidied over with green ground cloths. We boys stayed to watch four assigned farmers shovel the grave shut. Last, we raced to the church basement for a hearty meal of fellowship prepared by the Ladies Aid Society.

It was at such country funerals that doubts sprang to mind about the "sleep" state of an individual at death.

Everyone in church made the assumption that the human body and Soul body were one and the same.

Years later, I learned of other thoughts on the matter. Eckankar taught the fact of Soul's ability to leave the body in full consciousness at time of death.

Yes, the church held to its dark philosophy. The physical body, it said, would decay and serve as worm food, but on the Last Day a more glorious body would rise from the grave. That would mark Soul's victory over death.

But these tenets lent me little peace of mind.

What kid wouldn't have traded an eyetooth for a ringside seat at the cemetery on that last, great day? What a chance to catch the spectacle of a lifetime. Graves opening, and seeing all those people helping each other out of the ground? A splendid show. (Better than a county fair!)

Yet for all the promise of excitement, an ominous cloud threw its shadow over this one-of-a-kind presentation. What were the odds of this spectacle taking place in my lifetime? A million to one? No, a trillion. That left a most unhappy prospect. Would I be another of the billions and billions of unlucky Souls trapped in a dark prison hole for a thousand or ten thousand years? Not a bright and cheery picture for a kid with claustrophobia.

Moreover, what if something went wrong with the resurrection plan? Could it fail? What if I failed to awaken from the sleep of death?

Mistakes do happen.

So over time, funerals got more and more of my attention. You could say I was in search of a more secure plan for the afterlife.

I thus became a seeker.

Indeed, an awakening did occur as I grew from boy to young man. This awakening had stolen into my awareness like the first dim rays of a summer dawn and then burst into full glory some years later.

An early perception of God's love and grace had blessed me as a child. Like, what was that mysterious humming sound at night when I was two and three? My brother, two years older, and I still had a bed in the bedroom of our parents, so when my tiny voice pierced the darkness it awoke everyone.

"What is that?"

But neither Mother, Dad, nor brother could hear what I heard. When I tried to explain the "what" as a humming sound, they said, "It's only the electric wires outside. Now go to sleep." Dad's alarm would clatter at four o'clock in the morning to rouse him for chores. He had no time for nonsense from a kid.

Yet as the years rolled on, my thoughts at night would at times return to those early childhood memories of the mysterious humming sound. It had made me feel light, full, and good. Where had it gone? The electric wires still ran outside my window, but that soothing, almost musical, humming sound was gone for good, no doubt.

How wrong I was.

Later, in Eckankar, I learned that this humming sound was one of the many currents of God. It was part of the movement of God's Voice—the Holy Spirit, or ECK—vibrating the ethers of time and space to a level some ears could hear. Like, say, those of a child.

To listen to one of the sacred sounds is a great joy and spiritual blessing.

Anyway, a lot of gentle or stormy clouds had crossed the canopy of my life before that revelation about the humming's origin came to me. In the meantime, there were other awakenings too. Little ones, in looking back. Yet each was all I could accept at a given level of unfoldment. These awakenings included visions, dreams of past lives and the future, Soul Travel, and other spiritual experiences that left me wonder struck and sometimes even terror stricken.

Yet they spoke of the mysteries of the Eternal One, God, the Creator.

These small awakenings were directed at one goal: to find spiritual freedom in this lifetime. Here and now. There was no reason to enter a "death sleep" that could last for centuries, and maybe forever. What if my childhood religion had it wrong? There were a lot of other religions out there with conflicting beliefs. If my church had the wrong take on the life hereafter, I would wait in the grave a long time.

The joke would be on me.

\* \* \*

You are at that point, too, where some Voice of God has shaken you awake from a deep spiritual slumber.

I think you'll like the stories in these pages by people like you. You'll hear others tell a compelling story about a past life, a dream, or a Soul Travel journey that reveals the all-caring nature of God's love. This love works wonders.

Within this precious book are the voices of seekers like you, people also on the most direct path to spiritual understanding and freedom—here and now.

Welcome to past lives, dreams, and Soul Travel!

# Part One

## Past Lives

Most people on earth are returnees. The term for this recycling of lifetimes is the wheel of reincarnation.

# 1
# You Have
# Lived Before

six-year-old boy was seated near me, next to the window on an airplane flying over Louisiana. Looking down at the vast marshland with its many intersecting channels of water, he turned to his mother and called out in an excited voice, "It looks just like Ethiopia."

The embarrassed mother tried to quiet him. Everybody knows that Ethiopia isn't in the middle of a marsh, because drought has drained life from the place.

A businessman, sitting across the aisle from the boy, lowered his newspaper and began to chuckle. "Ethiopia!" he said. "Have you ever been to Ethiopia, boy?" He laughed, relishing the thought of any likeness at all between Ethiopia and Louisiana.

"It looks like Ethiopia," the boy said.

The man erupted into a bellow of laughter. Other passengers joined in. "The boy thinks Louisiana looks like Ethiopia," he said, repeating the boy's words for anyone who might have missed them. This brought a fresh peal of laughter.

The chastened boy grew quiet, and his mother flushed a bright red. When the plane was ready to

*"It looks like Ethiopia," the boy said.*

land, the boy said to her, "We're almost there."

"Where?" his mother asked.

The boy hesitated. Rather than say, "Ethiopia," he said, "There!"

The boy had recalled a distant past when certain areas of the world, now dry and brown, had enjoyed lush vegetation. His memory of those days was clear and certain. He remembered the past, because he had caught a glimpse from a higher spiritual vantage point. His eyes had glimpsed the Time Track.

## Wheel of Reincarnation

*Most people on earth are returnees. They've been here before, and they'll return another time.*

Most people on earth are returnees. They've been here before, and they'll return another time. The term for this recycling of lifetimes is the wheel of reincarnation. Karma, people's action and reaction in life, is its motor. The cycle goes on—lifetime after lifetime.

People of the Christian faith believe that when one dies, that's it. One life, one time, and then heaven or hell. They don't recognize the unchanging Law of Karma that nonetheless plucks them back to earth. They're on the Wheel of the Eighty-Four, a reference to the many thousands of lives that people enter in the lower worlds of matter, energy, space, and time.

It's a very dreary cycle. After a person recycles through many successive lives, a feeling comes that something's amiss with this scene, that something's wrong with the script. Then a thought creeps in. He begins to wonder about the "one life, one time" theory. Could it be in error?

He begins to grope for the truth.

It is common in today's media to come across some direct or indirect references to reincarnation. Some of the stories give a clear insight into it.

Yet how easy it is to dismiss a past-life story with, "Just another dreamer's tall tale." And it's a real temptation to discredit young children who give detailed accounts of past lifetimes. Even if it means ignoring the candid descriptions of settings, situations, and possible family ties of old. Yet this happens all the time in families with children up to five or six years of age. Take, for example, the boy on the plane, who recalled the Ethiopia of a greener age.

It's hard for some people in a Christian society to accept this information about reincarnation as a foundation for the miracle of birth. So they make up other explanations, that past-life claims are maybe some kind of mental transference. But wouldn't it be less of a problem to accept the simple fact of rebirth? Then you'd find sense behind the bounds of reincarnation.

Genius and disability are two quick examples of the influence of past lives.

People of religions other than Eckankar know and accept the principle of reincarnation. It's a principle of divine love in action.

Reincarnation allows people, like you and me, to have a chance to develop the quality of divine love. This opportunity comes through the hardships and uncertainties of life, as well as in the joys and fulfillment of living. So we develop the quality of divine love.

This love makes us more godlike beings.

*Reincarnation allows people, like you and me, to have a chance to develop the quality of divine love.*

### Awakening Your Past Lives

If you want a look at your past lives, the word to sing for a few minutes at bedtime is *Mana* (say MAH-nah). Then go to sleep as usual. This word attunes you with the Causal Plane, the region of past-life memories. Remembering past lives takes practice. But others do it, and so can you.

## Our Spiritual Wake-Up Calls

*Soul, when It came to earth this time, made an agreement with Itself to reach some goal and thus make head-way in spiritual unfoldment.*

Soul, when It came to earth this time, made an agreement with Itself to reach some goal and thus make headway in spiritual unfoldment.

Back in the 1930s, during the Depression, in a slum in Birmingham, England, a young girl of five set off for school. Let's call her Rose. She'd gone to meet her cousin, who would be excused from classes within the hour. All of a sudden, a golden light enfolded her. This golden circle of light was a spiritual wake-up call, and its glory sealed Rose off from the rest of the outside world. She could neither hear nor see others. But secure in the bliss of the moment she rested, content in the heart of this beautiful golden light.

Imagine a five-year-old child trying to gather words to relate an event of this sort. What adult would have given her two minutes? A celestial light of a half hour's duration that put all surroundings outside the realm of sight or sound? Go run and play, child.

You can see the difficulty. After a few such attempts to tell of the experience, Rose gave up.

Years later Rose decided to learn the nature of her youthful adventure. Thus began diligent research into past lives. By her midthirties, she had been an eager student of both Edgar Cayce and the Rosicrucians. She recalled ads in *Fate* magazine on Eckankar. Yet the search went on. She also studied Astara and Theosophy and read the books of H. Rider Haggard and others.

In 1972, Rose was startled by sightings of UFOs.

Along the way she'd become a devotee of three different branches of Buddhism. In quick succession came marriage to an executive in the movie industry and a family of three children. Rose also kept a busy social calendar. A fast-paced life, indeed.

Her agreement with herself from before this lifetime was on this order: to make a broad and thorough study of world religions and psychic groups. So she read books on every subject. In time, she gained a solid knowledge about the variety of ideas on truth.

Soul begins each lifetime with a clean slate.

The Lords of Karma erase memory of an individual's old mistakes, which allows for a fresh start. This kindness sidesteps a dead end. It avoids the error of someone taking up a new life and wasting it on past-life problems like revenge for a lost love, property, or social position.

Such memory loss is thus of benefit to Soul's progress. Then, somewhere along the line, Divine Spirit sends a spiritual wake-up call through one means or another.

The message is, "OK, it's time to remember why you came to earth."

Of course, the memory of one's spiritual mission is seldom relayed in such clear speech. Many go through years of doubt and uncertainty. They sample one religion or another, tripping from area to area in the occult field, or shifting from philosophy to psychology, even to mathematics. It's all in pursuit of the key to life and truth.

Sometimes a seeker makes few apparent gains but at some point says, "There's got to be more than this."

Some inner nudge leaves him unhappy with the knowledge so far gained. Some hidden impulse of

*The Lords of Karma erase memory of an individual's old mistakes, which allows for a fresh start. This kindness sidesteps a dead end.*

the heart drives him on in unending pursuit of God and truth.

> ### Past-Life Study Tips
>
> To awaken past-life dreams, make a list of people and things you like or dislike. Also note if you feel a special attraction to some country, locale, or time period in history. There is a reason for such interest.
>
> Now pay attention to your dreams.

## Coming Back

We used to have lots of cats on the farm. Every so many years there were three new kittens: one with gray-and-white patches, another with black-and-white spots, and a striped tiger kitten. Farm life was an unforgiving one, so they often translated (died) within a couple of years. Soon after, though, the same little group of three kittens came back in a new litter. Soul took a kitty's body until that body wore out. It would then leave for a while and sometime later return in a new cat body.

*When Soul can pass into a higher state of consciousness, into a more joyful world, It discovers a happiness that outshines every dream.*

The same principle of reincarnation holds in the case of family and friends who die and pass on. It's common to feel sadness at the loss—it's natural. But when Soul can pass into a higher state of consciousness, into a more joyful world, It discovers a happiness that outshines every dream. It is content in Its new state.

## I Knew You When You Were Old

A young girl accompanied her father to a retirement home to visit a great aunt. Arriving at the relative's room, they met the great aunt's roommate for the first time. Her name was Sophie. She was well along in years and close enough to the other side of life to catch a glimpse of life in those exalted places. Yet when she spoke of it to others, people shook their heads in resignation.

"Poor old Sophie," they said. "She's lost her mind."

The young girl walked into the room, passed by her great aunt, and headed straight for old Sophie. The two studied each other for a long time. Breaking the silence, Sophie, in a low voice, said, "I know you. I knew you when you were an old lady."

The little girl's clear gaze searched the woman. The look on the child's face said it too held a memory. "I knew you when you were a young lady," said the girl.

*The look on the child's face said it too held a memory. "I knew you when you were a young lady," said the girl.*

Two old friends touching bases.

The great aunt approached from across the room and patted her grandniece on the arm. "Don't mind Sophie," she said. "Her mind likes to wander."

How easy it is to discredit the wisdom of both age and youth by someone in the dark about reincarnation.

### WHAT PULLS YOU?

An attraction, say, to knights, medieval wars, and battles could be from a faint memory of past lives in some period of history. A Civil War buff, no doubt, saw military service during the tumultuous 1860s. That war left such a scar on the American nation that it still reveals itself as a deeply felt interest in Civil War history.

A child with a passion for model airplanes might have flown as an aviator in World War I or II, or even as a starship commander from Atlantis.

Someone with a feeling of ill will toward a

certain church or country for no apparent reason may once have been a victim of religious or political fervor. An ailment without a known cause, such as a chronic neck pain, may be a tip-off that a person was once hanged or beheaded.

Whenever strong loves or hates appear with no seeming cause, it means we are drawing the past into the present by agreement.

## Between Lifetimes

*Anyone in harmony with the true way of the Holy Spirit will demonstrate the survival factor.*

Anyone in harmony with the true way of the Holy Spirit will demonstrate the survival factor. It means doing whatever it takes to survive another day. Why make the effort? Because every second of life is a precious moment. Each day offers another chance to learn more about God's love.

Soul, at some point, will return to a new life on earth. No matter how hard Soul finds life, earth is an excellent place to learn the many dimensions of divine love.

Not just in the receiving of love, but in the giving of it.

\* \* \*

*The next two stories come from* Earth to God, Come In Please . . . , *Books 1 and 2. They offer a unique insight into occasions in which the ECK, Divine Spirit, gave ordinary people an extraordinary insight into truth. Read these accounts for a closer look at the miracles of life.*

### Checkers
By Doug Culliford

One child was six, and the other three. It was a preholiday gathering of family, and someone popped the question:

"What do you want for Christmas?"

"Checkers," replied the six-year-old girl. "I want checkers for Christmas."

"Checkers! Why, you don't even know how to play the game."

"Yes, I do!" the little girl said.

"Who taught you how to play checkers? Did you learn in school? Did your parents teach you?"

"Nobody did. We always used to play checkers." The girl's eyes were mirrors of truth.

"You and who else?" someone asked.

"My brother and I." The three-year-old brother looked up and nodded agreement to the questioning adults. "We used to play before, when we were big."

"Before? When was that?"

"When we were big before. Before we came to live here. We were old, older than you."

One adult consulted another. Minutes later, someone found an old, dusty box of checkers and set them up in front of the two children. Sure enough, the moves were familiar to them. They played like old hands. The adults looked on in bewilderment as the boy and girl nimbly moved pieces around the board.

"Did you live together before?" someone asked.

The little boy kept on playing, letting his older sister do the talking. "My brother and I lived in the same house then. We were married."

Someone mentioned a deceased uncle.

The little girl piped up, "I knew him too! I met him before I came here to live with you!"

This uncle had died before the six-year-old

*The adults looked on in bewilderment as the boy and girl nimbly moved pieces around the board.*

was born, and the doubting adults shook their heads at her fantasy. But she went on to describe him in perfect detail.

Now comes a curious thing. This family held to a particular religion that didn't acknowledge reincarnation. But over the years they had had many mysterious encounters with deceased relatives until, bit by bit, the family crossed the fine line between religious doctrine and actual spiritual experience. They began to acknowledge through the certainty of these experiences that reincarnation was not only possible, but probable.

And so they moved one step further from their limitations and a step closer to spiritual freedom.

*They began to acknowledge through the certainty of these experiences that reincarnation was not only possible, but probable.*

## Halloween Surprise
By Cameron Fox

The Halloween committee met every week for six weeks to plan the party for the hospital employees. We wanted everyone to have plenty of time to decide upon their costumes.

Many of the hospital jobs revolve around crisis intervention and other stressful life-and-death situations.

These parties are a time when all departments can share their lunch hour, dress up in bizarre costumes, laugh, and regain a playful, childlike spirit.

The music began promptly at eleven o'clock on the day of the party. Several committee members placed baked goods on the table to be judged. Then the judges—the hospital director, the dietitian, the chaplain, and others—went from item to item tasting the delicious-looking foods.

Hospital employees started coming in—many more than we had expected. The room soon filled with laughing people dressed in costume. This year the costumes were especially creative. One person, dressed as a bag of dirty clothes, had so many rags covering him no one could guess who he was.

After prizes were awarded for the baking contest, the judges took their places in chairs so they could see the contestants in costume as they walked across the stage.

The room was crowded with contestants, committee members, and other members of the hospital staff. All eyes were on the stage. One by one, contestants began to walk slowly across it, and some performed a skit to go along with the costume. Raggedy Ann did a short dance, the rock singer sang for us, and the soldier marched.

Finding a comfortable place to sit toward the back of the room, I closed my eyes for a moment and began a silent chant of HU, another name for God.

*I closed my eyes for a moment and began a silent chant of HU, another name for God.*

Singing this love song to God is something I often do. It gives a sense of peace and purpose, and lessens anxiety during a busy or stressful day.

After chanting for a few moments, I opened my eyes and gazed around the room. I had the feeling this might be a dream. Yet, looking down at my Gypsy costume, I knew it was not. I had dressed as a Gypsy every Halloween for years. As a child I had even performed in a chorus of Gypsy dancers for a ballet recital.

Closing my eyes a moment, I saw a vivid picture. It was much like a picture postcard.

There appeared a vision of me dancing around a fire with others dressed like Gypsies.

By choosing this outfit again and again, I was stepping back to a time in the eleventh century when I was learning lessons of survival as a Gypsy.

Many times in my job as a counselor I am called on to assist patients to find meaning in their lives. This requires teaching basic survival skills such as physical, mental, and environmental health. As a counselor, I am often among highly emotional, even unpredictable people. This does not upset me.

I learned survival skills and an ability to balance uncertainties during that Gypsy lifetime. They continue to be useful to me even today.

Sitting in the back of the room, I felt as if I were surrounded by light. That light projected to five other coworkers in the room—the gorilla, the pilgrim, the cat, the Indian, and the soldier. Of all the costumed workers, these were the most comfortable and believable in their roles.

Had they chosen their costumes for the same reason I had chosen mine—for the chance to step back into the past?

When these contestants took their turns upon the stage, everyone in the room applauded. The judges, too, were obviously impressed. These five were each awarded the top prize—dinner for two at the best restaurant in town.

Halloween has taken on a whole new meaning! It will never be quite the same for me again.

> *I learned survival skills and an ability to balance uncertainties during that Gypsy lifetime. They continue to be useful to me even today.*

You are the sum of all your thoughts, feelings, and actions from this life and every lifetime in the past.

# 2
# Past Lives, Present Lessons

dd as it may seem, you had a special reason for coming into this lifetime. It was to become a more godlike being, but most people do not realize this fact. They assume that birth is a fancy of destiny.

*I'm here; I don't know why,* they think. *Bad luck, maybe? Troublesome place, this.*

All in all, earth is nothing other than a spiritual school. God designed and set up this place so that you and every other Soul here may develop godlike qualities and thus become more like God.

Many people think they exist to fill time and space until the trumpets sound on that last day. Then, having lived a fruitless, selfish life, they expect to fly to some higher world, to continue a useless, self-serving life there as well.

Not so, me hearties.

No, indeed. The purpose of life is to become a Co-worker with God. It means service to others, using our talents and interests to give hand, ear, or heart to another in need.

All the lives you have ever lived were for the polishing of Soul. Like it or not, you are now at a

*The purpose of life is to become a Co-worker with God. It means service to others, using our talents and interests to give hand, ear, or heart to another in need.*

17

higher and more spiritual level than in any prior incarnation. So look at yourself. Do you like what you see? Keep in mind, whatever it is, for better or worse, it's of your own making.

You are the sum of all your thoughts, feelings, and actions from this life and every lifetime in the past.

*You are the sum of all your thoughts, feelings, and actions from this life and every lifetime in the past.*

## Past Lives Are Tied to Karma

Sometimes people ask, "What does Eckankar have to offer that's unique? How is it different from Christianity?" So I may speak to them of karma and reincarnation.

People, in general, think of karma as an unpleasant force and less often as having a beneficial side. Take for example Mozart, already composing music at age five.

The rule of karma determines factors like male or female body, eye-hand coordination, long- or short-term memory retention, and desires. In addition, our karmic package includes race, ancestry, family, friends, economic and social standing, and much more besides.

However, what comes of those conditions depends upon the exercise of our free will.

The Law of Cause and Effect, or the Law of Karma, is always in play your whole life. You must know how to live in harmony with its exacting terms. The experiences that derive from an adolescent or mature understanding of that law will, in time, bring you to an acceptance of divine love. That's the reason you're here.

## Family Karmic Groups

In the 1890s, a young girl and her six brothers and sisters came by ship from Europe to America.

A fever struck during the voyage across the Atlantic. It cost the lives of her siblings. All were lost.

This girl arrived in America, grew up, and later married. She had six children. These returning Souls were the brothers and sisters who had perished on the voyage from Europe. Being such a tight-knit karmic group, they kept incarnating with each other.

Years later, one of these children died in an accident. He reincarnated four months later as the son of one of her other children. Many noted the boy's resemblance to his deceased uncle. When the boy grew to manhood, he stayed around the family home, doing repairs and taking care of the family members as he had before as the uncle.

Only two of the six children in this woman's family ever married. Since they were such a close karmic group, most of them preferred each other's company to that of others.

When these Souls find Eckankar, this family karma will begin to melt. They will work through traits and conditions that have bound them to each other for many lives, and so again move on in their spiritual lives. Karma may create a net of fear. These Souls carried a fear of life, the reason for the inseparable bond that stretched back for centuries.

Yet when love appears, fear must flee; love brings freedom.

## Good and Bad Karma

People like to think of karma as bad. Yet there's a balance between the good and bad; it's the way of spiritual law. Overall there is as much good karma as bad—but one or the other enjoys dominance at a time.

For this reason some people are without a home. Others bask in wealth. A homeless person may be

*People like to think of karma as bad. Yet there's a balance between the good and bad; it's the way of spiritual law.*

selfish or generous, while the same traits hold for a wealthy individual. This example suggests a tension between the making and dissolving of good and bad karma.

*The scale of divine justice weighs all karma. Its measure is exact.*

The scale of divine justice weighs all karma. Its measure is exact. Every thought, word, and deed stands naked in the court of divine judgment.

## Insight into Another Life

A group of students from Ghana traveled to another country for a year's study. They wanted to become more fluent in French.

One of the girls, a black student, happened to meet a white German man. Soon they were close friends. Her acquaintances started to talk.

"Got a romance going?" they asked. "With a whitey?"

When someone of a different race, nationality, or even habits breaches the established order of a community, many times it's a recipe for trouble. Eyebrows are raised, and fair-weather friends run up their true colors. So her friends began to spread rumors and pass falsehoods about her friendship with this white German male. The girl wished to lose neither her friends from Ghana nor her new white companion.

She debated about the best course to take. To soothe the ferment, she sought counsel in a spiritual exercise.

It's easy to do a spiritual exercise. Shut your eyes and imagine a conversation with your spiritual guide, whomever you feel comfortable sharing the secrets of your heart with. It can be Jesus or some other religious figure. ECKists look to the Mahanta, the Living ECK Master, the spiritual leader of Eckankar.

So in a spiritual exercise, this young woman said, "Please, Mahanta, give me an insight into this. What can I do? I don't want to lose my friends on this side or my friend on that side."

Such was the concern she laid before the Mahanta.

In the next instant she became aware of being in a past lifetime, standing on a shore with a baby in her arms. Close offshore stood a slaving ship. White men dotted the beach. They brandished whips at a line of black slaves ranged along the sand, shackled in chains.

*In the next instant she became aware of being in a past lifetime, standing on a shore with a baby in her arms.*

A point of interest: news media report cases of one race accusing another of atrocities. Cruel and inhuman treatment is the charge.

Yet many black people once sold into slavery in Africa were prisoners of war of another black tribe. The conquering tribe had a choice. It could either kill the defeated warriors or trade them for money or goods. In spite of the heartless nature of the choice, it did forestall an immediate death.

Their captors thus delivered them from the interior of the continent where the white men were loath to venture because of malaria and other diseases.

In sum, the fighting between black tribes took place inland. Then the victors marched the captives out and sold them to slavers, who shipped the unfortunate Souls to ports in North or South America. Those voyages saw the most brutal conditions one can imagine.

But revisionists want to rewrite the historical record. Years later, they alter history after the backdrop of those times has been forgotten. Agitators, they twist events to fit a modern personal or political fad. One claim is that all atrocities were the fault of only one party to the action.

Such a revision of history is meant to deceive. It foments new strife.

In this woman's past-life experience, white men herded blacks onto the ships while she watched in tears, with a child at her breast. Her husband was one of the slaves. She begged the slave masters, "Please let my husband go. We have a child." Her plea brought harsh laughter.

Soon the last line of slaves boarded the ship. As they embarked, her husband cried out, "If we don't meet again in this lifetime, surely we will meet in another."

*When this inner experience had ended, the Mahanta said to her, "Your friend in this lifetime was indeed your husband then."*

So the ECKist from Ghana realized it wasn't mere chance to have met this white German student and develop such a strong attraction for him. It was a past-life connection. She also began to notice an oddity. Whenever he was with her, he behaved like an African. He walked, talked, and gestured like an African.

She used to observe him and wonder, *Now where did he pick that up?*

When this inner experience had ended, the Mahanta said to her, "Your friend in this lifetime was indeed your husband then."

Finally, she understood the strong rapport between them.

After this she could better handle the faultfinding of her friends, who tried to intimidate her by saying, "You shouldn't be seen with that white man. What will people think?"

This criticism was the voice of the social consciousness speaking. It's an element of the human state that tries to put everybody within a society at the same level. It abhors a taller head in the crowd and attempts to pound all heads to the same social, financial, or philosophical level. This social consciousness is the great leveler. Its spiritual harm comes in its frantic zeal to stamp out individuality.

After this inner experience she drew a firm line with her friends, because now she knew the origin of her affinity for the white German. He was a dear friend from the past. And there she took a stand.

### TRAVEL BENEFITS

As you travel to new places, dreams may reveal some past lives you spent there. Such dreams shed light on habits, likes, or fears. They show things gained or lost ages ago. Travel is thus a chance to revisit the foundation of what helped make who and what you are today.

So take a trip and be aware.

## Past-Life Lessons

During my first years in ECK, I had the good fortune to experience many past-life recalls. Some were pleasant. There were also a number of unpleasant ones, recalls of lost opportunities in reaching some desired goal. Not memories to celebrate in the least.

Yet each lifetime, even a supposed failure, gives a fuller understanding about your spiritual nature. You learn about yourself as a spiritual being.

Soul is immortal. It has no beginning or end. It (you) exists because of God's love for It, which is the whole philosophy of Eckankar in a nutshell. Our mistakes in this and past lifetimes are the polishings of a precious gem in the rough.

*Soul is immortal. It has no beginning or end. It (you) exists because of God's love for It, which is the whole philosophy of Eckankar in a nutshell.*

The definition in Eckankar of Soul as an immortal being is a valid one. Soul, created in the timeless worlds, existed before birth and endures beyond time and space. God made Soul before the worlds of time and space began. Soul comes to earth from the higher spiritual worlds to add to Its experiences. It inherits many lifetimes for the chance to learn.

And learn It must.

*Soul, created in the timeless worlds, existed before birth and endures beyond time and space.*

* * *

*The next three stories are also from* Earth to God, Come In Please . . . , *Books 1 and 2. Listen to Dennis Calhoun, Debbie Kaplan, and Beverly Foster tell how the subtleties of karma played out for them.*

### God, Who Should I Marry?
By Dennis Calhoun

In college I met a woman, a sure marriage partner. From the first moment it seemed we had always been together, but after graduation, she found a job in Chicago. I landed in Houston. So we kept up a long-distance relationship.

One day during a spiritual exercise I told the Inner Master, the Mahanta, of my desire to marry.

I explained the need for companionship. If the ECK (Divine Spirit) could work it out, and if it were for the good of everyone, well, that would suit me fine.

Months passed with no resolution to our situation. So we decided to date other people, because it didn't seem likely that I could transfer to Chicago or she to Houston. Soon after, I met a woman, Jaye, and we began to date.

Four months later my company made a big announcement. It would open an office in Chicago, and the plans called for my transfer there.

*Perfect!* I thought. I had let go of concern with the situation, and the ECK had opened a way for me to move to Chicago and marry my college sweetheart. But before I left Houston, Jaye shared her feelings with me. She believed we belonged together. She was certain I felt something for her too—and I did.

But in my mind, in my thoughts, I was headed for my girlfriend in Chicago.

After arriving in that city, I soon became engaged. Our relationship was peaceful and calm, as if we had been married before. But then, things began to fall apart. Somehow, our plans to marry no longer felt right to either of us, so with heavy hearts we broke off the engagement.

Once again I took the matter into contemplation. The answer was clear: follow your heart. Go see Jaye.

So far, I had followed my head and that hadn't worked out. So I called Jaye back in the Houston area. A wonderful feeling rushed into my heart, and I knew I wanted to marry her. But I still didn't understand the reason.

Wasn't it too big of a decision to make purely on the feeling in my heart?

Jaye and I took a trip to New Orleans about a month before the date set for our wedding. While on a walk, we discussed some wedding details. In the French Quarter we turned a corner. Dumbstruck, I stared into a breathtaking courtyard.

That one moment showed me an entire past-life experience.

I turned to Jaye in astonishment and saw that something had happened to her too. We

*I took the matter into contemplation. The answer was clear: follow your heart.*

began to talk. Imagine our surprise to discover we'd both had the same vision of a shared past life!

During that incarnation in the late 1850s, I had been a young man in the southern United States. In about 1859, I moved north to find a job to pay for medical school. There I met a northern woman (my college sweetheart in this life). We married. Her parents were wealthy and put me through medical school. Soon after, the Civil War broke out. I returned to the South to serve as a doctor for the Confederacy.

While stationed in New Orleans I met a woman (Jaye, in this lifetime), and we fell in love. But I was married, so we did not act on our love.

Then the war came to an end.

I left New Orleans and returned to my wife in the North. Jaye and I never saw one another again, and I spent the rest of that life living comfortably with the woman I almost married in this life.

After the brief glimpse of this past life, I understood why my relationship with my college girlfriend had been so easy. We had been married before. It also explained why I thought we should marry again. The mind likes familiar and comfortable paths. Still, my heart needed fresh experiences and growth in this life, so it wanted to move on and fulfill the love left behind in New Orleans in that life. Jaye and I have been very happy in our marriage.

*Now if I hear two voices—one from my head and one from my heart—I know which is guidance from Divine Spirit.*

Now if I hear two voices—one from my head and one from my heart—I know which is guidance from Divine Spirit. The heart is more often aligned with Soul, the true self.

Thoughts are from the mind. The mind is a

good servant, but a poor master.

Now I always tell my friends, "When in doubt, follow your heart!"

## A Deadly Race against Time
By Debbie Kaplan

A few months before attending an Eckankar seminar, I had a disturbing dream. In the dream I was at the seminar, running to the main auditorium. I opened the doors and looked inside— and every single person in the auditorium was in a wheelchair!

Upon awakening, I couldn't figure out the dream, but I recorded it in my dream journal.

Life went on. About two months later my husband offered to buy me a very nice weight-lifting machine. I accepted his offer, and two men came to my home to set up the machine. It turned out that the proper handlebar for the machine was missing. The installers gave me a bar from an older machine. "It'll be OK," they said. "Use the old bar, and as soon as the new one comes in at the shop, we'll send it out to you."

They left, and I started to try out the machine. Within the first five minutes the handlebar slipped from the machine. My foot was almost severed from my leg.

For one long moment, time stood still.

I stared at my leg. Then I saw the Mahanta standing next to me. Without words, he told me it was OK. This "accident" was a result of karma from another life. I would be all right.

Things happened fast after that. The ambulance I called whizzed me to the hospital. As the surgeons reconstructed my foot, they told me

*I saw the Mahanta standing next to me. Without words, he told me it was OK. This "accident" was a result of karma from another life.*

that I was lucky to have survived. But, as Soul, my attention was on the deeper reason for this event. I had to know why. What karmic tie had brought about this horrible accident? I asked the Inner Master to show me a fuller picture of the true cause-and-effect relationship at work in my life.

I discussed some of my dreams, which held the clues to my injury, with a Higher Initiate in Eckankar. As he listened the picture became clear.

*On the path of Eckankar one can work off tremendous amounts of karma in the dream state and through the daily Spiritual Exercises of ECK.*

The karma that caused my injury was with the two men who had delivered and set up the machine. Two lifetimes ago I had caused them similar misfortune which led to their deaths.

I, as Soul, had chosen this lifetime to repay the debt for that transgression against the spiritual laws of life. As I looked further at the past-life records, it was clear that the accident was meant to end this lifetime.

But the Mahanta had interceded on my behalf.

On the path of Eckankar one can work off tremendous amounts of karma in the dream state and through the daily Spiritual Exercises of ECK. Unwittingly, I had been in a race against time. Yet through the grace of the Mahanta, the Inner Master, he had lifted enough of the karmic load so the accident wouldn't cost my life.

Looking back, I realize that I had had a burning desire to study Eckankar for three or four years before becoming a member. Now I know why. It was a race against an internal clock. With five small children it would have been hard for them if I'd left this life so soon. Now I'll get to see them grow up.

It was also a relief to understand my wheelchair dream—that's my mode of transportation these days. However, I'm very hopeful of one day walking again.

I'm forever grateful to the Mahanta for the protection and help necessary for me to stay in this life for more spiritual lessons, love, and growth.

## Getting Off Spiritual Welfare
By Beverly Foster

It looked like I had finally used up all my miracles. My husband and I had always lived on the borderline financially. If we had money, we spent like kings. If we didn't, we lived like paupers.

In between, we did our best to control our finances, but we couldn't seem to figure out a way. During those years we leaned on the Holy Spirit. Sure enough, each time we were headed for disaster a miracle intervened.

One year I quit a well-paying job. We hadn't planned how to make our house payments, but my retirement savings and gifts from my family added the needed amount to my husband's income. A few years later my husband started his own computer business. One project was to develop a piece of software. At the same time I changed careers to freelance writing.

From then on whenever we faced certain financial ruin I would sell an article or someone would call from out of the blue to order a computer program. Bonuses at work, unexpected inheritances, gifts when most needed—the evidence mounted to prove that God was taking care of our every need.

One summer we were perched about as far

*Bonuses at work, unexpected inheritances, gifts when most needed—the evidence mounted to prove that God was taking care of our every need.*

out as possible on the usual cliff. This time, though, the miracles were slow in coming.

I'd quit my job, and now we faced another financial crunch. With luck, if I found a way to make some extra money, and if we could control our spending a little more, we might survive. If not, there was a good chance we'd miss the next house payment.

I awaited a sign from the Holy Spirit that all the good ifs would become reality when I went to Sunday's worship service at the Temple of ECK. Sri Harold Klemp was the speaker. Excited, I closed my eyes and opened my heart to him.

"Are we going to be better off now?" I asked inwardly.

He'd know what I meant.

Then I sat back for confirmation of my hopes. Instead, three words in his talk went straight to my heart.

"Tighten your belt."

While Sri Harold (the Outer Master) spoke this from the stage, the Mahanta (the Inner Master side of him) added in a loud voice to my inner ear, "This means you!"

Certainly the sign I'd been waiting for, but not what I wanted to hear.

I headed straight for my office after the service to look over our finances. Grimly I asked myself where to cut spending. We had almost stopped buying new clothing. We never went to movies. We only ate out in restaurants once in a while. I shopped at the cheapest grocery store. What else could we do?

As it turned out there was plenty. I added up every paycheck for the next six months,

*I went to Sunday's worship service at the Temple of ECK. Sri Harold Klemp was the speaker. . . . Three words in his talk went straight to my heart.*

subtracted the bills, then divided the balance by the number of weeks. That was the amount we could spend. No more. The only way to meet our bills was to stick to this plan. At the end of five months we'd be caught up. There'd be extra money for Christmas.

For the first time in our marriage, we had a budget.

Actually, the figures in the budget were quite generous. My husband's income was more than adequate for our needs, but living within it would be hard. And we got no breaks. The kids continued to wear out shoes at a horrendous rate. Nor did we lose our appetites for those occasional pricey restaurant meals, but this time no surprise checks or lucrative job offers came to soften the blow. Still, we managed to stick to the budget—no matter how tight it seemed—for all five months.

At the end of that time it occurred to me to ask the Inner Master what I had done to create this lifetime of financial problems. The answer came gradually through my dreams and contemplations.

One morning before my spiritual exercise I asked the question again: What had I done to create this lifetime of financial problems?

I closed my eyes and sang HU, a love song to God. Opening my eyes to my inner vision, I saw a beautiful young woman before me. Her blond hair was cut short in the bobbed style of the day. Green eyes were smudged with dark eyeliner.

In a gentle, almost childish voice she spoke of the corrupting influence of money.

"Look at my father," she said. "He used his

*One morning before my spiritual exercise I asked the question again: What had I done to create this lifetime of financial problems?*

money for power and didn't care who got hurt in the bargain."

I could imagine the cruel and capricious parent who had oppressed this woman beyond her limits. To escape, she had run away to finish that lifetime in the gutters of Paris.

When I realized this woman was me in a past life, I could go back and forth between her world and mine, seeing the truth from both points of view. While I had enjoyed the benefits of great wealth in my youth in that lifetime, I had not appreciated them. Wealth was like air, or water, or my own beauty. It was always there. When I did allow myself to think about it, it was with feelings of guilt for having so much while others had so little.

In my contemplation I could see the many opportunities for wealth squandered in this lifetime. The many times I had relied on others to care for me. Relinquishing control over money had absolved me of responsibility and guilt.

So I spoke to the woman, showing her how her attitudes had traveled through time to restrict me in this lifetime. She was in full agreement.

Then she pointed out how my fear of poverty could in the same way prevent me from having valuable experiences in a later incarnation. Surprised, I had to admit she was right. Poverty taught sacrifice and discipline, while abundance brought lessons in discrimination and giving with love. Together we had eliminated these extremes. But in so doing we had thereby wedged ourselves into a very narrow corridor of few new experiences.

We vowed to remove all restrictions.

*When I realized this woman was me in a past life, I could go back and forth between her world and mine, seeing the truth from both points of view.*

I came out of contemplation with a great sense of relief.

The cushion in our budget is a little softer now, but things have not changed all that much. We still need to watch our spending. After years with our hands out to Divine Spirit, it's not been easy. But each step toward financial independence brings a greater pride in our own abilities.

So at a time I despaired of miracles, I received the greatest one of all—proof that the Mahanta's love could teach me to stand on my own two feet.

This experience had broken the old karmic chain. It allowed the girl to move ahead in her spiritual life and never have to return to earth.

# 3
# Remembering
# Past Lives

hy remember past lives?

We need to understand that the challenges we face today involve all sorts of past-life experiences. Once we gain awareness of these links to other lives, it's possible to handle our challenges in a better way this time around. We can end a chain of karma that has hung on for centuries.

All debts must be repaid before one gains spiritual freedom.

A man in Africa was grieved to learn that his young daughter had died without warning. The mother had taken the child to the hospital for a minor illness, but the head nurse had administered the wrong inoculation. So their daughter passed over to the other side.

The father was distraught. He demanded that the owner of the hospital and the head nurse explain the reason for his daughter's death.

"What have you done?"

"We didn't do anything wrong," they said. "The medicine didn't work."

Yet the answer rang false. In a disturbed state of mind, he found it hard not to strike the nurse in

*We need to understand that the challenges we face today involve all sorts of past-life experiences.*

anger and frustration.

The day of the funeral arrived. All the neighbors in the community came to offer condolences. The link between families was a very strong one in that community, and the people had come to help bury the dead child.

As the parents mourned at graveside, a beautiful golden butterfly hovered over the crowd. Then it flew away. As the father looked closer at the dirt around the grave, he spotted a caterpillar. He realized that Soul going into a higher state is like a caterpillar transforming into a butterfly. During the time this butterfly had attended the melancholy gathering, the father also noticed a flock of white-and-blue birds—about a dozen—flying in a circle over the crowd.

In spite of these two spiritual signs of a higher purpose to all this, he remained distraught. He went home and wrapped himself in a sheet. Then he began to sob.

In his grief, he cried, "Mahanta, why did you allow my daughter to leave like this?"

Soon thereafter he fell into an exhausted sleep. While asleep, he met the Mahanta, who came to him and said, "Have you learned nothing from the ECK teachings? My son, I have tried to teach you, and yet you carry on like a child."

The scene changed.

In a room that appeared stood his daughter. She ran up and hugged him. After they had hugged awhile, she began to squirm, wanting to get down, run off, and play.

Then the Mahanta spoke again. "Just wait a minute. Let me show you something. Please hold your daughter."

*While asleep, he met the Mahanta, who came to him and said, "Have you learned nothing from the ECK teachings? My son, I have tried to teach you, and yet you carry on like a child."*

Like magic, a TV appeared on the wall, and a movie began to play.

The Mahanta said, "We are now going back to the Oracle at Delphi."

As they watched, a scene formed on the TV screen showing five warriors locked in mortal combat. Two of the warriors were the parents of this girl. His daughter was also in the fray. The scene revealed her as a very strong enemy warrior in that lifetime, and she overpowered two of her parents' tribe. But two warriors—now husband and wife — overcame this powerful warrior (their daughter).

The Mahanta explained the scene.

"In that lifetime," he said, "your daughter was the very strong warrior who killed these other two in battle. One of the warriors is the owner of the hospital. The other is the head nurse. If you had struck the nurse in the hospital, she would have died and this would have extended the karma for another round."

"The only way to resolve this karma," the Mahanta added, "was for your daughter to pay it back here. That would release her from her last life on this earth."

Then the father realized that this collection of characters—himself, wife, daughter, the owner of the hospital, and the head nurse—were not casual strangers. They had been together in that earlier life. The scale of karma was thrown out of balance then. Yet this experience had broken the old karmic chain. It allowed the girl to move ahead in her spiritual life and never have to return to earth. She was now full of light and joy.

As to the reason for her appearance as a warrior in this past-life replay, the Mahanta said, "That is how you knew her."

*"The only way to resolve this karma," the Mahanta added, "was for your daughter to pay it back here. That would release her from her last life on this earth."*

Now she had the freedom to go on to a higher and happier place.

Once he saw and understood that, the man awoke and told his wife the dream. They could still grieve the loss of their child, yet it was now possible to understand the reason for this apparent injustice. They realized that her death was justice after all. True justice.

Then they found peace.

*They could still grieve the loss of their child, yet it was now possible to understand the reason for this apparent injustice.*

## Learning about Ourselves

Some years ago on my first visit to Paris, I roamed this fabled city where Roman conquerors had set up a colony at a busy crossroads in 52 BC. It became the capital city of the Franks in the sixth century. In the eighteenth century it lay at the center of the French Revolution. Then, in World War II, captive of the Nazis. Paris today remains the glamorous belle of Europe.

In the airport a woman in her sixties shared a remembrance with considerable pride. No doubt drawing on rich memories from the Second World War, she said, "No single man is safe in Paris. I ought to know—this is my town!"

She'd not been a nun.

Paris had been my town, too, on more than one occasion in recent incarnations. The last major lifetime there was during Napoleon's ill-fated march on Moscow in 1812.

Napoleon had marshaled six hundred thousand troops and crossed the Russian border in June, but by October the Russians had forced his retreat in the biting cold of winter. Only fifty thousand French soldiers escaped the Russian regulars. The rest died.

Along with other young men of France, I had been compelled to leave wife and home for war. There was no choice in the matter. All able-bodied men received orders to join Napoleon's vast military forces.

The march into Russia began in the summertime, but we saw little of the enemy—except for the major battle at Borodino in September. It was a phantom force that liked to slip away before a major face-to-face encounter.

All through history, the Russian winters have proved a stout ally to the Russian people. Hitler, the reincarnation of Napoleon, tested his luck again in World War II with the same disastrous results. His armies suffered a rout as convincing as did those of Napoleon in the earlier campaign.

In late autumn, I fell to a grave illness outside Moscow during the ragged retreat of the French army. Here my last days in that lifetime were attended to by a young Russian woman whose family tried folk remedies to restore me from a bout with pneumonia. In this life she is my daughter. All attempts at recovery, though, failed as frostbite ate at what little health remained.

Napoleon had underestimated the enormity of supplying his large army with food and clothing.

As a consequence I left that life a disillusioned man. His shortsighted plans were at the root of our bad luck. They caused my untimely passing. Our summer uniforms, in tatters after the harsh summer campaign, were a thin joke to the Russian bear of winter.

I brought two strong feelings into this life from that period in the early nineteenth century. One is a distaste for cold weather. The other, a respect for

*Along with other young men of France, I had been compelled to leave wife and home for war.*

leaders who draw up careful plans before launching big projects.

## Character Building

Many people do not know the fact of Soul's rebirth into a succession of lives on earth. Few learn to recall past-life memories so that lessons of long ago can be recaptured for advantage today.

Most run their lives as if this stay were a one-shot deal—the beginning and end of all that's worthy of reflection. Yet is it a crime to say that Soul inhabits a physical body but one time? Or that It never chafed under a master's discipline in a past life? Or that It never took on other incarnations at the death of those bodies, to see rebirth today and advance Its spiritual education?

No, it's not a crime to be ignorant of divine law. Experience is a hard-nosed teacher; time, the great educator.

Our character is made up of virtues and shortcomings, and all are a development from past lives. A reason lurks in the background of every twist of personality. Each trauma from a forgotten life shapes our conduct in a given way. Without exception.

Unless, of course, the force of Divine Spirit enters our consciousness to override the mind's knee-jerk reaction to life's challenges.

Divine law is the beginning and end of all truth. That law includes karma and reincarnation.

*Experience is a hard-nosed teacher; time, the great educator.*

### KNOWING

When an unexpected situation comes up, you might be surprised you know what to do. In dealing with it, you enjoy a sense of knowing the right steps to take.

Where does this knowing come from?
In a past life, you may have ministered to
others as a medic on the battlefield. At some
level you carry those memories with you. So
when a sudden emergency arises and by second
nature you sense the right thing to do, you may
be drawing on experiences from the past.

## Beginning to Recall

A woman in New York City we'll call Amber has
had a fear of icebergs since childhood. To travel from
one area of her city to another means a ride on a ferry,
and she dislikes boat rides. Nor does she care to swim
near rocks. On one vacation in Puerto Rico, the tide
had caught and swept her out to some rocks, where
she went into a panic and came near drowning.

She'd often wondered about this fear of rocks in
water, and her intense fear of boats.

The fear grew in strength as Amber reached
adulthood. By then she noticed an absolute terror
when seeing even a picture of icebergs.

What would cause such a response?

At one of her Eckankar classes, the group tried
a spiritual exercise to view the past. As they did the
exercise, she wondered, *Is it possible that I was on
the* Titanic *when it sank in 1912?*

Amber went into contemplation to find out. She
did begin to see into the past. Yet before allowing an
outcome, she cut off the experience and sat waiting
for the others to finish the spiritual exercise.

The next night at bedtime she did her usual
contemplation. The Mahanta came and asked, "Why
did you cut off the contemplation yesterday?"

"I just felt uncomfortable, and I didn't want to
see any more," she replied.

*As they did
the exercise,
she wondered,
Is it possible
that I was on
the Titanic
when it sank
in 1912?*

"It's important for you to see and know what's happened in the past," the Mahanta said, "so that you can live this life without fear."

*"It's important for you to see and know what's happened in the past," the Mahanta said, "so that you can live this life without fear."*

## *Titanic* **Memory**

So Amber went into contemplation a second time that evening. The Mahanta, the Inner Master, let her see the past like a movie, as if she had become an actress in this movie. She was indeed booked as a passenger on the *Titanic.*

But she didn't die on the ill-fated maiden voyage of this famous ship. She was a survivor. One of the women to secure a seat in a lifeboat, she was thus able to save her life. Some men in the water wanted to climb into the lifeboat, but she fended them off. She feared it would sink and threaten her own life.

In this lifetime Amber gave birth to two healthy children, but after these full-term pregnancies she had four boys in a row who died soon after birth. Each lived just a few hours to a few days. Then they died.

What was the reason for this string of heart-aches?

In this contemplation scene, Amber saw that her refusal to let the drowning men into the lifeboat was a most selfish act. It denied others the right to live.

That was the reason for her loss of four sons.

A second realization was that in the previous life she'd been born into a selfish family, a family that scorned generosity. And she proved to be the most selfish of them all.

With that understanding of her past, Amber could choose a new direction in this lifetime, one of love and service to others.

## Our Karma at Birth

When fear is a dominant player in your life, it steals the joy and freedom of living.

Hidden fears—stacks and stacks, piles and piles of them—reside in each human being. What is their origin? Many fears developed before your birth into this lifetime. Each human being carries a history of hundreds or thousands of past lives. That allows plenty of time to hurt others. And it also gives them a chance to hurt you. Get hurt enough in a certain way, and you cringe from the mere thought of that sort of pain.

People are not born equal. At birth each brings a unique load of karma.

But most people have no idea how to work it off. How many even know it exists? And so they cower inside their coats of flesh, too afraid to live and too scared to die. They desire heaven; earth is hell. Yet they fear the passage to heaven, because the passageway is death.

It's the mother of ironies.

*People are not born equal. At birth each brings a unique load of karma.*

## Spiritual Opportunity

Maybe your life has been anything but easy. For all of us life dishes up hard knocks, because they get the job done. It's the best way to learn our spiritual ABCs. The expansion of consciousness finds fertile soil in hardship.

Like you perhaps, I had my share while growing up. They continue today. Life will crush you, unless you rise above them.

We do whatever it takes to keep strong, to retain our health. We employ our God-given talent of creativity and the ability to listen in order to flourish in every area of life. We do all within our power to thrive. This incarnation is a gold mine, a rich life, worth every ounce of trouble that rebirth brings. And should we abuse the trusts and responsibilities in our care, we learn of better ways in the hot furnace of karmic burn-off. The heat of life teaches us that some things don't make it. In the end, the only thing that counts is love divine.

We come to a conclusion. It's not knowledge, we realize, but a *knowingness* of divine love that holds the key to wisdom and spiritual freedom.

*The heat of life teaches us that some things don't make it. In the end, the only thing that counts is love divine.*

## Subconscious Memories

Angry people often spoil for fights of tongue or fist and thus risk a shortened life. The next time around, their conscious memory of past lives is a clean board. Otherwise they'd return with an eye toward gathering sticks, stones, and knives, all the quicker to assail old foes with a vengeance.

That said, however, the subconscious memory of past events does remain.

It is the intuitive memory of past-life deeds of wrong or right. You carry this memory, as we all do to one degree or another.

The subconscious memory of past rights and wrongs done to us explains the reason you may walk into a new job and feel good, right at home. The people seem like old acquaintances. In fact, they are. You knew them in happy circumstances before. Again, the subconscious memory may cut the other way. You could land in a place where someone takes delight in slipping burrs under your saddle. For no known reason. You and Joe Gruff start off on the wrong foot, because you sense he's behind a plot to unseat and send you out the door.

And you could be right.

## Around the Wheel

The subconscious memories of past experiences with associates are but a small portion of the human family's grand circle of karma.

Within the larger circle of human karma, which includes all people of all nations, myriad smaller circles exist. These include still lesser groups. All in all, we find the people of the individual nations, states or provinces, cities, towns, and neighborhoods in the ring of human karma.

In the smaller and most important circles of karma are the intimate realms of friends and families.

In Wisconsin, my birthplace, one was bound to bump into a second or third cousin everywhere within thirty miles of home. Everybody knew everybody. The broad family is a strong karmic group. Yet family circles of karma also cross national borders, into the domains of other governments, where foreign laws set a different tone of interaction upon relatives there. These larger circles of Souls all rest upon the immediate, the nuclear, family. And within this tight group—husband, wife, and children—opposing states of thought and action pose a day-to-day challenge.

Why the strife? A family is an intimate group that learns spiritual grace by its members bumping into each other, thereby smoothing over rough edges.

Various scenarios play out within each family circle. In one case, a boy may suffer mistreatment by his father. So when the boy grows up, he mistreats his own children. Time sees him grow old, weak, and helpless. Then an adult offspring, who has the care of him, may relish the opportunity to return the favor and neglect the old man's needs.

*A family is an intimate group that learns spiritual grace by its members bumping into each other, thereby smoothing over rough edges.*

And so enmity takes an ever firmer grip and perpetuates itself into another generation.

Still, all meet again in the future to face each other, in mixed roles, eager to continue the ages-long karmic battle. So father may return as girl, mother as father, boy as mother, plus the happy mishmash of some uncles, aunts, and cousins tossed into this karmic salad.

That's the way of karma.

Friedrich von Longau, in *Retribution,* caught the spirit of karmic action in the human arena. He writes, "Though the mills of God grind slowly / Yet they grind exceeding small."

There is no way off this wheel of reincarnation until each person learns about the Light and Sound of God. They lift the individual above the petty self, above human nature.

*There is no way off this wheel of reincarnation until each person learns about the Light and Sound of God.*

* * *

*The following story is from* Earth to God, Come In Please . . . , *Book 1. Mr. Spaulding shows how the Mahanta helped him resolve a sticky karmic situation with his employer. Things turned much worse before they got better.*

### A Business Challenge
By Ed Spaulding

My job was going well. I was a salesman for a printing company and had landed a number of large accounts. My commissions were increasing every month, and I was happy and excited about the future.

One day the owner of the company, Dave, called me into his office. "Ed," he said, "I want you to sign a new contract." It retroactively lowered commissions which he had yet to pay me. I would lose over ten thousand dollars. The new contract also put a limit on my future earnings.

When I voiced a protest, Dave said, "You're making more than your job is worth. I have to restructure your commissions."

In shock at the sudden turn of events, I muttered something about needing time to look over the contract, then stumbled from his office.

I put off signing the contract for several days. The more I tried to negotiate with Dave, the angrier and more intimidating he became. When I sat down to do my spiritual exercises, I realized I was caught in a web of emotional and mental turmoil. Trying to talk with Dave was draining me. I was hurt by his unwillingness to communicate. At last, he gave an ultimatum, "Sign the contract, or you're fired!"

I realized I didn't trust him anymore. How could I then keep working for him?

Within myself I began to sing HU, the love song to God, to keep in balance. I said, "Dave, I quit. But I want to be paid what is owed me according to the old commission structure."

Dave flew into a rage. His face turned as red as a beet. He shoved me out of the building, and I felt lucky to escape without injury.

As I drove away I felt relief. But he'd cheated me out of a lot of money. So terrified was I of Dave that I didn't know whether it was worth the trouble to go after my lost commissions.

Partly out of avoidance and partly because of needing a break from the tension, I stopped thinking about the situation. I calmed down and soon began a new business in another area of the printing field.

One day, while driving to my new office, I

*Within myself I began to sing HU, the love song to God, to keep in balance.*

noticed a large rusty car trailing me. Waves of fear and anger washed over me. Dave was having me followed. A game of cat and mouse ensued as I let the other car pass and then tried to catch up with it, but it escaped in traffic.

Later, looking out my office window, I saw the same rusty heap at a stop sign. My heart began to pound. I chanted HU to myself, asked for divine protection, and ran out to confront the driver. Questioning my own sanity I knocked on the window of the rusty car.

*Questioning my own sanity I knocked on the window of the rusty car.*

The man swore at being caught. He rolled down the window and shouted, "I should be beating you up right now."

In my most calming voice, I said, "Why is Dave paying you to follow me?"

"Dave says you're out to destroy his business. He told me you needed to be watched. He even offered me a two-hundred-dollar bonus if I would beat you up!"

I stared in openmouthed amazement. He continued, "My brother said you were a nice guy. He knows you from work and advised me not to do it." As the man drove off, I stood wondering, *Why has my life suddenly transformed into a bad TV movie?*

There was no avoiding Dave now. My anger was stronger than my fear. I called and said, "You better stop having me followed!"

He denied everything and instead accused me of stealing his customers. If I didn't stop, he would sue me. Hanging up the phone, I realized it was time to see a lawyer. I needed to know my rights. Picking a law office out of the phone book, I made an appointment.

The night before going to see the lawyer, I

had a vivid dream of being back in Dave's office. His wife came up to me, her face filled with fear and desperation. "Please, Ed," she said, "don't you and the lawyer put us through this again."

She even mentioned a lawyer's name.

Then Dave came up. "I'm going to sue you!" he said.

To my surprise, though, he didn't try to throw me out of the office. Instead he said, "As long as you're here, the least you can do is help out." He was working on a job I'd once sold for him, so I joined in.

To make the job work, I had to fold up the contract he'd wanted me to sign and wedge it under a chart to keep it from slipping.

The dream shifted. Now I was in my home, where the same piece of paper came back from Dave in the mail. On it was written the amount of money that would settle our differences.

Then I awoke. I wrote down the dream and felt encouraged. But it was time to rush off and meet my new lawyer. When I arrived, it was a shock to discover that the attorney on my case had the same name Dave's wife had spoken in the dream!

Showing the lawyer my documents, I described the situation. His eyes lit up with dollar signs.

"This will be an easy case to win," he said. Perhaps he sensed some reluctance on my part, because he added, "I'll even waive the normal retainer to get us started. Just sign here."

Instead, I just sat there. My thoughts returned to my dream and what it meant.

It seemed that if I sued Dave, it would be a repeat of an old play from a past life. If there were only another way to work things out.

*The dream shifted. Now I was in my home, where the same piece of paper came back from Dave in the mail. On it was written the amount of money that would settle our differences.*

Then, our karma would resolve once and for all. So I asked the lawyer for time to think things over and left.

Later, in contemplation, I spoke of my frustration to the Mahanta. I asked to see the past life that had caused such intense conflict between Dave and me.

The Mahanta said, "You'll see these past lives in time. For now, I'll arrange a meeting with Dave, Soul to Soul, to begin to work out your karma."

*In my contemplation the Mahanta opened a door. In walked Dave, smiling and full of light.*

In my contemplation the Mahanta opened a door. In walked Dave, smiling and full of light. It was great to see him happy and willing to talk. Here, in a higher state of consciousness, we shared the goal of resolving all karma between us.

So I asked him about the behavior of his human consciousness.

"I'm afraid of you!" he said.

This was amazing, since I was afraid of him. I then asked, "Well, how can we work things out on the outer, since I can't speak with you?"

Dave smiled and said calmly, "A way will be provided."

I thanked him and the Mahanta, because now I was beginning to feel things could work out.

A few days later I received a very threatening letter from Dave's lawyer. But at the end of the letter it said to call him if I had any questions. "Aha!" I cried. "This is the way Dave has provided for communication."

The meeting with my lawyer had convinced me I was in a position of legal strength. So I called Dave's lawyer and explained my case to him. I told him all I wanted was the commission owed me. Later in the day Dave's lawyer called back. Although he'd obviously had a rough session with his client, he had convinced Dave to pay me in full!

For the next year, I received monthly checks from him in the mail. This monthly income enabled me to sustain myself while I built my own business, a goal I'd had for some time.

I realized that the experience with Dave had strengthened me. It had given me the courage to take the risk of forming my own business. Next to the risk of enduring a new difficult boss, starting my own venture seemed easy.

After a year, Dave's lawyer called. "Dave's willing to meet with you to reach a final agreement," he informed me.

Preparing to call Dave and set up an appointment, I realized I was still terrified of him. So I went into contemplation and met him again, Soul to Soul.

I asked, "Would you please tell me what you need to keep your composure when we meet?"

When I called Dave, the first thing he said to me was, "We'll sit down and go over the books. But I can't handle any discussion. Please respond to me in writing."

I realized this was what he needed to keep his balance, so I agreed. There were two tense meetings. I kept my promise not to argue with him in person, so we resolved our differences on paper, struck an agreement, and went our separate ways.

Shortly after our last meeting I had a vision. I saw Dave and me in a past life where he had cheated me in a business situation. I had responded in a vindictive manner, ruining his

*I realized that the experience with Dave had strengthened me. It had given me the courage to take the risk of forming my own business.*

business. In a moment it was clear that Dave's tremendous anger in this life was a mirror of my own hatred from the past. It was coming back to me in the present.

To work off the karma for ruining his old business, I helped Dave build his present company into a success. When he cheated me in this life, it was a golden opportunity for me to grow spiritually. I could work things out in a balanced way, while facing my own anger at myself and him from the past.

In forgiving Dave, I was forgiving myself.

A year and a half later I ran into Dave on the street. To my surprise, instead of getting into his car, he came over. He smiled and shook my hand.

"Just after our last meeting I had a severe heart attack," he said. "I nearly died. The doctor told me I had to sell my business if I wanted to live."

Dave had spent the past year traveling around the world with his family, having a wonderful time. He commented, "It's great to get to be the nice guy in life. My only regret from the business was how I treated you."

Quietly, Dave apologized to me. I accepted his apology with tears in my eyes, and we were both swept with a wave of emotion.

*I felt the presence of the Mahanta. With it came the knowingness that, at long last, our karma was healed.*

I felt the presence of the Mahanta. With it came the knowingness that, at long last, our karma was healed.

As I looked into Dave's eyes, I recognized the beautiful Soul I had met on the inner, now outwardly manifested.

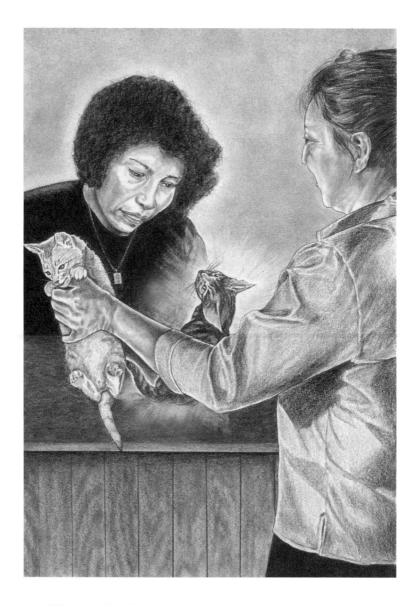

"A male?" she said. "My cat was a very feminine female. I can't imagine her coming back as a male cat."

# 4
# Death as a
# Continuum of Life

woman we'll call Lana kept a female cat for a pet. They'd lived together for eleven years and enjoyed a strong love bond, but in time the cat died. Of course, Lana missed her long-time friend.

About a year after the cat's passing, Lana noted a series of clear dreams.

In one dream, someone said, "Your cat will reincarnate on Monday, July 31." When Lana awoke, she thought, *That dream was nice, but I live in an apartment in a big city now. I don't know how my cat will find me.*

Then came a second dream.

In this dream someone handed her two kittens. Both kittens were striped; one was lighter, the other darker. The Mahanta, the Inner Master, said, "The darker of the two is yours."

That same week one of her friends called. "Two of my cats had litters at the same time," she said. "Would you like a kitten?"

When Lana went to look at one of the litters, she saw the striped kittens from her dream. "This is my cat," she said, picking up the darker of the two.

"It's a male," said her friend. Lana paused. "A male?" she said. "My cat was a very feminine female. I can't imagine her coming back as a male cat." She felt a sudden unease about her dream.

But her friend said, "If you want a female, there's a lovely gray-and-white kitten in the other litter. This kitty loves everybody." But it didn't love Lana. "I think I'd better stick with the striped one," Lana said, releasing the clawing bundle of fur.

On her way out Lana asked, "By the way, what was the mother cat's name?"

"Z," came the reply. (Z is another name for the Inner Master, Wah Z.) As she drove home, she thought, *Maybe this really is my cat, even though it's a male.*

Later, for contemplation, she opened an ECK book at random. It read: "Soul will alternate between male and female bodies, each time learning some lessons while gathering karma and working off karma."

Lana had her answer. The striped male kitten was her old friend come back.

*Soul will alternate between male and female bodies, each time learning some lessons while gathering karma and working off karma.*

## Fear of Death

The greatest fear of all is the fear of death, say pundits.

They avow that everything about it has already been said. That is true in part. However, the poetic Preacher of Ecclesiastes had an eloquent way of placing death in perspective with the experiences of life. "To everything there is a season," he said, "and a time to every purpose under the heaven: A time to be born, and a time to die. . . . A time to weep, and a time to laugh; a time to mourn, and a time to dance."

We think we know the meaning of detachment until one of our own passes to the other side. Then we're not sure. We wonder, *Where is God in this our sorrow?*

The philosophers of old grappled with the matter of death too. Epicurus, the Greek philosopher of the third century BC, taught that the physical senses are infallible in determining truth. What a misunderstanding. Yet he did make an interesting point.

"There is nothing terrible in living to a man who rightly comprehends that there is nothing terrible in ceasing to live," he said.

Lucretius, the Roman philosopher and poet, felt that death should be of no concern at all. When Soul leaves the body, he said, It ceases to exist. Life is swallowed up in death.

A hopeless and gloomy philosophy if ever there was one.

But the searing light of truth as taught in Eckankar is like a flaming arrow, because it pierces the shell of such grim philosophies. Eckankar teaches the freedom of Soul. Soul triumphs over death. It is a spark of God. Its very existence rests upon the divine breath of Holy Spirit, the ECK, the sacred Light and Sound.

*Eckankar teaches the freedom of Soul. Soul triumphs over death.*

Therefore, Soul is the victor; death, the vanquished.

Now consider birth.

Birth is the miracle by which Soul enters a new physical body. It's the opening chapter of our life, while death marks the last. But death's victory is brief. Our first cries as a newborn, like the probing fingers of dawn, herald an awakening from a night of rest.

Soul is eternal. That is Its heritage. Through

ageless cycles of the miracle of birth, Soul continues Its quest to become more like Its Creator. It's like a bee that must find the nectar.

An individual matures, then dies; his atoms return to dust. Yet before ages pass, the Lords of Karma stir the dust to create a new body for him. And so he begins another round on the wheel of life.

Death is thus a passing from one chapter of life to another, and from there to still another. The process is a natural one. It's been a part of your experience many times in the past. But you can stop this cycle. The teachings of ECK show how you too can find spiritual freedom in this very lifetime.

*The teachings of ECK show how you too can find spiritual freedom in this very lifetime.*

## Seeing Death from Above

An acquaintance told of an out-of-body experience he'd had in his early forties. For the sake of privacy, we'll call him Andy. A heart attack struck him down. Then an ambulance rushed him to the hospital where doctors did everything in their power to save his life.

In the middle of all the confusion, Andy had left his body. Hovering near the ceiling like a pair of eyes, he felt a great happiness. There was no concern about the fate of his pale physical body stretched out below on the operating table. Then a doctor injected a potent drug. A powerful force drew him back to his unconscious body, though he had no desire to return to it.

Later, Andy told a nurse of this out-of-body adventure in the operating room while his body lay unconscious. But none of the staff put much stock in his story.

At last, he decided to keep the experience to himself. The medical staff was giving him odd looks, because they feared his mind had suffered damage from a lack of oxygen.

* * *

Another ECKist recalled a similar story about his dad, whom we'll call Carl. Carl told his children about the time a serious illness had brought him to a hospital in critical condition. Carl told this story so that his children would not go through life with a fear of death.

Here's what Carl told them.

His heart had stopped beating. A doctor had no luck in trying to start it. All this happened years ago, before medical knowledge had advanced to its present state. The family vet happened to be present. He hammered both fists on the stricken father's chest, trying to restart the failed heartbeat.

Carl, in the meantime, went outside his body. From a point near the ceiling, he enjoyed a commanding view of the whole scene. He watched the frantic attempts of the two doctors below.

Then his attention switched to a new scene. He found himself climbing a spiral staircase. An enchanting melody beckoned him on, ever higher up the stairs. There was no desire to return to his body. Then he faced a doorway, sensing that if he passed through it, his earthly life would end. So he started for the door. It seemed like a gift from heaven.

In desperation, at that exact moment, the veterinarian dealt his chest the sharpest blows yet. This enraged Carl. The extreme pounding was drawing him away from the doorway that promised a life of eternal peace. He awoke, railing and cursing. The doctors and nurses supposed the outburst to be a case of delirium and so ignored him. Patients did that sort of thing.

*He found himself climbing a spiral staircase. An enchanting melody beckoned him on, ever higher up the stairs.*

After this Soul experience, Carl lost all fear of death.

What an upbeat story to pass along to one's children.

But let's return to the hospital now for later evidence of Carl's out-of-body experience.

One of the doctors had lost his pen during the excitement brought on by Carl's crisis. When Carl confided to a nurse what had occurred while his body lingered near death, she dismissed his tale. Imagine her shock when he told her where to locate the doctor's pen. None dared believe his story. However, they were hard put to explain how he knew the location of the lost pen, which had eluded the medical staff's best attempts to find it.

Carl is not a member of Eckankar. But his son, who told the story, has been a member for some years.

"My dad isn't a member," he said, "but as far as he's concerned, Eckankar makes more sense than a lot of that other stuff."

Take it from one who knows.

\* \* \*

*Both of the men, each having had an experience of being outside the body, are strong individuals.*

Both of the above men, each having had an experience of being outside the body, are strong individuals. Fears of sin or guilt don't trouble them. They take responsibility for their thoughts and actions. Nor do they bend to pressure to become a member of one religion or another. They know their own minds.

A disguised threat like "Join us or risk damnation" is fire without heat—of no effect at all.

In early American lingo, these two are salts. They have crossed the creek and scaled the mountain.

A large number of people in the United States claim at least one vision. This category may include a strong, unforgettable dream or an out-of-body experience.

Whatever form the experience takes, it is a wake-up call from God.

From that time on, many become seekers. Yet they may continue this lifetime in the church of their youth, unwilling to upset a family or social framework by leaving that community of worshipers for Eckankar. Many acknowledge, however, that Eckankar does offer more real answers to spiritual questions than does their church.

So they are seekers.

Perhaps in the next lifetime, they will muster the courage to embrace truth. They will pose the age-old questions that all seekers ask: "What is my purpose? What is the meaning of life?"

Then the Master appears.

## Your Destiny as Soul

Soul enters this world to pursue a series of tasks, for each is an exercise in spiritual purification. Taken as a whole, these assignments make up one's destiny. To set the tone for Its mission, Soul enters a new lifetime with a body of strength, or weakness; into wealth, or poverty; of great intellect, or a simple mind; in a popular shade of skin, or not; either as a male, or a female.

The idea of destiny as a concept is out of fashion in much of today's Western society. People want to be captains of their own lives. They wish to run their own fate. They will shape their own tomorrows. Yet how can they do so without a knowledge of and an appreciation for the meticulous Law of Karma?

*Soul enters this world to pursue a series of tasks, for each is an exercise in spiritual purification. Taken as a whole, these assignments make up one's destiny.*

Or especially, of the Law of Love?

In spite of all fictions about who is the master of their own fate, they cannot even set the conditions of their birth. And so the rules of karma and reincarnation remain a mystery, and they find a great deal of sorrow and disappointment in the outcome of their plans.

How could the stiff rules of karma include them?

Many would like to think they don't, sure of being above the common pool of humanity and thus exempt from these rules.

By and large, though, the Lord of Karma—not the individual—selects a family for each Soul. Soul must then follow the script of destiny and enter a physical body.

The Lord of Karma is like a minor's guardian. He administers a trust on behalf of a spiritual infant, arranging for him or her to join a family with the best prospect for that Soul's unfoldment. In selecting the time and place of reincarnation, the Lord of Karma is the sole judge. He is the sole arbiter in the choice of a body, health, family, or future. The Lord of Karma alone sets the conditions of most people's fate.

Placement is a simple karmic detail. The Law of Karma governs all such placements, and he is only its agent.

The primal seed for each incarnation exists under the umbrella of destiny, which we also call past-life karma. On a practical level, genetic, cultural, and social elements combine to decide Soul's place in this world. For people on the lower end of the survival scale, the Lord of Karma alone chooses the time and place of rebirth.

After birth, then, the name of the game is sur-

*The Lord of Karma is like a minor's guardian. He administers a trust on behalf of a spiritual infant, arranging for him or her to join a family with the best prospect for that Soul's unfoldment.*

vival. The survival scale, by definition, is a measure of one's can-do instincts.

But karmic placement does set other standards for individuals on the high end of the spiritual scale. More of them enjoy a voice in the choice of a human body or place of birth. They sense the need for spiritual freedom, a view gained from many past lives, and the self-responsibility that goes along with the package. So these Souls demonstrate creative ideas and inventiveness in their incarnations. For the most part they are cheerful, upbeat people.

Spiritual gains in past lives have given them a voice in choosing some of the conditions in their present incarnation.

They have earned the right.

Think of destiny as the equipment, talents, or gifts that one brings to this life. They carry a divine mandate to use them for the good of all life. It's our responsibility to do so, with wisdom.

The idea of destiny, or fate, is poked fun at in many Western circles. Yet it is an age-old principle of the spiritual life.

What is the basis for a cultural bias against fate?

People are in a state of confusion about it. They wonder, *How can fate and free will exist side by side?* Destiny controls the conditions at birth. Much of what an individual does after birth is an open book, an exercise in free will. Free will can offset or even overcome the drawbacks of destiny, but only through the awakening of one's consciousness. One may thus reshape both his material and spiritual life.

To sum up, fate governs the conditions at birth; free will allows a choice as to how to move beyond them.

*Think of destiny as the equipment, talents, or gifts that one brings to this life.*

## Lessons from Each Life

A past life was a moving force in teaching you compassion for others, even though in that life you showed no empathy for the suffering of others. At times, perhaps, playing the role of torturer, cruel lord, or even terrorist. A later life, then, to restore balance to the karmic scale, demanded you suffer the indignities of a victim. So you become the tortured, the oppressed, and the violated.

It's all in the game.

*Each lifetime teaches at least one lesson and often dozens.*

Each lifetime teaches at least one lesson and often dozens.

Of course, other lifetimes were routine ones. With no monumental lessons, they nonetheless served as an opportunity for healing and reflection. You may have jockeyed from an early lifetime of adventure to a later one of rest. People do return to earth to heal. They squirrel away in a quiet place in some pastoral setting, a token reminder of the heaven they left behind.

Bless the likes of hermits, shepherds, and homebodies. They have their place.

## Learning about Love

A European man told this story about his elderly father and mother.

One day the father, call him Aaron, suffered a stroke, and an ambulance rushed him to the hospital. Recovering in a few weeks, he returned home though still weak.

Soon thereafter came a second shock. Doctors found his wife had a terminal illness and gave her but a few short days. She was comfortable with life yet showed no fear of death. She took the news in stride. She told Aaron not to worry, then entered a hospital. The doctors, who'd been witness to similar crises in other families, were astounded by her serenity.

During the final days of separation, husband and wife missed each other, of course.

Then Aaron's mate tried an experiment. She used an imaginative technique to be with her beloved. Later she explained to her son that she simply imagined herself at home in bed with Aaron. The first night of her experiment, Aaron woke the next morning and told his son an odd thing.

"Your mother was here beside me in bed last night."

The son, an ECKist who understood the ways of Divine Spirit and knew of the love bond between his parents, expressed his happiness for them.

The few precious days passed. The couple often shared their nights in this way, and soon Aaron began to hear a celestial Sound of ECK. He confided to his son that he had never heard the songs of birds with such clarity. He could distinguish the birds by their songs.

Yet, in fact, these sounds were not of earthbound birds at all, but from the Holy Spirit, or ECK. The Voice of God was manifesting to him like birdsongs. It was the off-season for such birds.

Aaron's wife translated, or passed on, ten days after she entered the hospital. Before her passing she made a last visit to him in a dream, in some heaven on the inner planes. She said she would not see him for three days, she'd be busy with experiences on a number of inner planes.

But she'd return.

She explained the whole matter in a way he

*These sounds were not of earthbound birds at all, but from the Holy Spirit, or ECK. The Voice of God was manifesting to him like birdsongs.*

could understand. Dying was like moving to a new state or province, so she'd be collecting such things as a driver's license and vehicle registration, new lodgings, and the like.

On the fourth day after her death, Aaron awoke and spoke to his son.

"I saw your mother last night. She was young and beautiful and dressed in her nurse's uniform the way she'd looked when we met during World War II."

A short time later the son, passing his father's room, noticed his sister by their father's bedside and so entered the room. Aaron opened his eyes.

"It's all right," said the son. "It's only me."

But Aaron looked beyond him. As if seeing someone else enter the room, he opened his eyes wide in amazement. They told of neither fear nor dread, but of joy. At that very moment he slipped from his body in peace, joining his dear one in the green fields of heaven.

The radiant smile on the father's lips was testimony to love's transcendence over death.

The son felt deep gratitude for the chance to witness his father's passing from his tired and worn body. This occasion marked a turning point in his spiritual life too.

The joyful experience of attending his parents' passing taught him many lessons about the power of love over all things, including death.

*Aaron looked beyond him. As if seeing someone else enter the room, he opened his eyes wide in amazement.*

## A Series of Steps

Life is a series of steps. We lurch from point to point, in one lifetime, then another. Such a period in time may offer excitement, burnout, or any other state—whether it should endure a lifetime or an hour. Then again, pleasant and quiet intervals will grant seasons for reflection and contemplation, to give leisure to glance ahead or back, to take stock of lessons in our schooling.

A period of reflection or contemplation awakens a yearning for truth. It will rouse a more fervent desire for love.

Then the teachings of ECK appear.

Life and death have no real boundaries. Death is but a gateway, yet life encompasses all things. In Eckankar, we learn to live, move, and have our being within the grand sea of life's endless rhythm.

On occasion, little beams of warm sunshine illumine the cold, dark moments of our lives. This sunshine is God's love. When we let its warmth into our hearts and minds, it routs darkness and fear. When love has conquered all our fear, we have finished the need for future lives on this planet. We rise to a higher state. We are able to bask in the greater blessings of our Creator.

And so the power of karma and reincarnation is reined in.

More spiritual freedom is ours.

*  *  *

*Dee and Kathie recount true stories about the mysterious link between life and death. These accounts are from* Earth to God, Come In Please . . . , *Books 1 and 2.*

### Pop's Reincarnation
By Dee Meredith

As a member of Eckankar I often wondered how to prove reincarnation to myself. Were my

*In Eckankar, we learn to live, move, and have our being within the grand sea of life's endless rhythm.*

flashbacks of previous lives just imagination?

Some time ago, my father translated (died). I didn't attend his burial service but was honored to be present inwardly as he awoke in the Astral world. Before long he was up and about, learning about his new home in the inner worlds.

Ever so often I would stop in during my spiritual contemplations to see how he was. It was amusing to find that the spiritual principles we had discussed before his death were becoming a reality for him now.

These inner visits went on for about ten months. But one day when I stopped by to chat with Pop, he wasn't in. At first I thought he'd just gone off to explore and would return. But when I asked the Inner Master, he said Pop was preparing for another incarnation on earth. I was surprised but realized that as Soul, Pop must continue on.

One day at work I heard a soft voice inside telling me to watch for my father's incarnation in a few months. I wondered about this. I couldn't think of any woman I knew who was pregnant.

Then I remembered meeting a young couple just after my dad's translation. We'd become fast friends; I felt I had known them for years. She was pregnant now, and I had a knowingness that Dad would return as her baby.

I went to visit my friend the day she came home from the hospital. Everyone was crowded around the baby when I arrived. Catching my first glimpse of the newborn, I noticed his physical structure was like my dad's former human body. The child had the same unmanageable

*When I asked the Inner Master, he said Pop was preparing for another incarnation on earth.*

fine hair and yellowish complexion that ran in our bloodline.

In silence, I welcomed this Soul back as I picked up the baby. With intent alertness, his little untrained eyes made an effort to focus on me. I touched his Third Eye with my forefinger. A golden light radiated outward and engulfed his entire head, as his three-day-old baby face twisted into a lopsided grin of recognition.

He strained to move his vocal cords. With a great effort he screamed out my nickname! His new parents were speechless. A ripple of love spread through the room, and we all began to laugh.

In that moment, a wealth of information passed between the baby and me. It was an instant swapping of information, Soul to Soul. One thing I sensed was that Dad felt scrunched up in that tiny body!

I keep track of this Soul through his parents. When I drop by for a visit every so often and he hears my voice, a familiar, lopsided grin brightens his face in welcome.

*I welcomed this Soul back as I picked up the baby. With intent alertness, his little untrained eyes made an effort to focus on me.*

## A Special Feeling of Love
By Kathie Matwiv

I work as a nurse in a terminal ward. Patients die there every day. As an ECKist, I have a golden opportunity to practice divine love and compassion.

The first time I met Mike, I knew a karmic link had brought us to this place. Feeling a strong, unconditional love for him, I wanted to make his last days as comfortable as possible.

One day I was wiping his face as he slipped in and out of consciousness. *What past life,* I wondered, *brought us here?*

Looking at his face while relaxing and thinking of the Mahanta, I heard the distinct report of single-shot rifles. My Spiritual Eye opened. Then I saw myself as a young soldier being shot in the chest.

Another soldier, whom I recognized as Mike in this life, ran to my side. He lifted me over his shoulder, carried me to a ditch, and spoke to me of God as I died.

Now, in 1992, our positions were reversed. The brief vision explained my special feeling of love for him. When he died a few days later I was there, singing HU and telling him of the divine Light and Sound and the Inner Master, the Mahanta. I was even given the opportunity to comfort his mother and brother.

How great the joy to repay a debt of gratitude with true spiritual understanding.

*How great the joy to repay a debt of gratitude with true spiritual understanding.*

If a problem or question troubles you, try this exercise to see if its roots are buried in a past life.

# 5
# Spiritual Exercises
# to Recall and Resolve
# Past Lives

any of our dreams relate to past lives. Once we come to that realization, we can begin to access the experiences that lie hidden within our memory banks. And, yes, it is possible to bring hard-won lessons from past lives into the present for a better understanding of our situation in life today.

What are the means of accessing this wealth of experience?

Begin with one of the easy spiritual exercises given in this chapter.

The key to the knowledge and wisdom gained long ago in the school of hard knocks is inside you. This key is true desire. You must want to make spiritual headway when embarking upon a study of dreams to profit from your past lives.

So what is the heart of this quest to be?

Let it be a true desire to become a better human being.

Love and mercy are the stuff of life. A study of dreams has the power to open your heart to the essence of your real self. Who are you? These spiritual

*A study of dreams has the power to open your heart to the essence of your real self.*

exercises can help you reach out to learn the answer and find the secret to self-mastery.

Read the spiritual exercises that follow. Then choose for practice the one with most appeal to you. Work with it. See where it leads you.

Later, do the same with each of the other exercises.

### The Movie Screen Method (To Find Your Inner Guide)

Find a comfortable position and relax. Shut your eyes. Now look at an inner screen, and imagine you are viewing a movie screen. It may be black, white, or even gray. In time, a lifelike scene or moving picture should appear.

Look right at the screen. After a while, let your inner vision shift a bit to either the left or right of it. From the corner of your eye, look for any movement on the screen.

*This is a useful method to search for your inner guide.*

This is a useful method to search for your inner guide.

In a relaxed manner, then, look off to either side of the mental screen, knowing full well that your attention is, in fact, on its center. Now sing HU or some other holy name of God.

Do this spiritual exercise while singing HU, for it starts a purifying, cleansing action within you (Soul). Old habit patterns like a lack of confidence, idle chatter, fear, and self-deception will begin to lose their hold on you.

Watch love replace them.

### The Sherlock Holmes Technique

If a problem or question troubles you, try the following exercise to see whether its roots are buried in a past life.

First, shut your eyes. Then, in your mind's eye, imagine Sherlock Holmes sporting his funny-looking, double-billed cap. Jump-start your imagination by visualizing a luminous blue shape. Watch it crystallize into the tall, lanky form of Sherlock Holmes with a magnifying glass in hand. He's coming along a path. As the detective draws near, you see that he is, in fact, the Mahanta, the Living ECK Master.

He greets you, then says, "If you'll come with me, we'll find a solution to your problem."

Take up his offer and accompany him. The incredible blue light about him is like a dazzling shield. You note that the light passing through his magnifying glass acts like a flashlight. Together you enter a misty marsh.

The Blue Light of ECK illuminates the path.

On this walk with the Mahanta, chant the word HUUUACH (HU-akh). It's similar to HU. This word goes with this exercise. Continue to walk with the Inner Master, who, you recall, is dressed like the famous detective.

Soon, an enormous rock blocks the path. The Mahanta, still dressed as Sherlock, lifts it without effort. He holds his magnifying glass for you to see through. The blue light shining through the glass turns white. There, emblazoned on the bottom of the rock, you see the solution to your problem.

*See what discoveries await in the secret hollows of your being.*

Do this exercise every other night for a month, switching it with your usual spiritual exercise. That will bypass the resistance of the mind.

See what discoveries await in the secret hollows of your being.

### The Radio Announcer Technique

Do you feel there are mislaid pieces of information about some aspect of your life—for example, a disturbing dream or a problem—that feels like a link to a past life? If so, try this technique to help fill in the missing pieces.

Go into contemplation. That means, shut your eyes but open your heart and mind.

Now listen for a Sound of ECK. It may be any common, familiar sound. Or, there may be silence too.

Visualize turning on a radio. Next, imagine an announcer's voice filling the airwaves. Listen to him sum up the highlights of the dream or problem whose meaning is unclear to you.

*Then imagine the radio announcer saying, "And now, here's the rest of your dream."*

Sing HU for a few minutes to relax. This pause is like taking a commercial break.

Then imagine the radio announcer saying, "And now, here's the rest of your dream." Let him fill in the missing pieces of the dream and thus unravel its meaning.

In the case of a bad or frightening dream, you can be sure the dream censor has not allowed the whole story to come out. So begin with the assumption that something is missing. You don't know all the details. Then let your inner faculties get the answer via this Radio Announcer technique.

A solution could come during this spiritual exercise, but it may appear later in a dream. Again, you may awaken with a clear understanding of your dream or problem.

So be aware.

### The Formula Technique

Like so many other ECKists who practice contemplation or enjoy dream travel, I'd have adventures on the inner planes. But how to tell where the experience took place? Was it on the Astral, Causal, or Mental Plane?

Of course, these planes differ in spiritual importance to us. However, when an inner experience did occur in my early years in ECK, I was often at a loss to tell in which spiritual region it took place.

One night the ECK Master Peddar Zaskq gave me a technique to determine one's location in the other worlds. "It's like a visitor's pass to a certain plane," he said. "Anyone can use it, whether a First Initiate or a Fourth. Instead of just letting the experience happen and then hoping for a signpost later, here are four exercises to help you discover your location in the higher worlds."

Then he gave these four exercises of the Formula Technique.

The Physical Plane, he said, is the first level of existence. Right above it lies the second, the Astral Plane. The Causal Plane is third in line. The Mental Plane is next.

Formula Two (there is no Formula One) is for explorations on the Astral Plane, the second level. Chant HU, the love song to God, two times, then breathe twice without chanting HU. Continue this technique for fifteen minutes before bed or in contemplation. All the while, lightly hold in mind your desire to see and explore the Astral (emotional) Plane.

Ask the Mahanta, the inner guide, to show you an important past-life record from a previous life on the Physical Plane. It may shed light on mood swings, likes and dislikes, and unreasonable fears.

Formula Three is ideal for the third plane, the Causal. Follow the same procedure as for Formula

*Ask the Mahanta, the inner guide, to show you an important past-life record from a previous life on the Physical Plane.*

Two, except now chant three times and breathe three times (without chanting HU). This plane contains the seed of all karma. Before falling asleep, imagine yourself on the Causal Plane at the Hall of Records. It is a repository of past-life records on the Physical and Astral Planes, the two planes below the Causal.

Formula Four is for the fourth plane, the Mental. Chant HU four times, then breathe in a normal way four times. This plane is the home of math, architecture, philosophy, higher ideas, and arts along this line.

Formula Five is for the Soul Plane: five HUs and five breaths. The Fifth Plane is the dividing line between the lower, material planes and the higher ones of pure Spirit. It is also the place of our Soul records, a detailed account of our past lives on all the lower planes—the Physical, Astral, Causal, and Mental regions.

Before you begin an exercise, write in your dream journal which exercise of the Formula Technique you will try. After you gain a degree of success with an exercise, begin to compare all experiences from the same plane. See the common thread woven through each of them. Note the unique texture of experiences on the Astral level in comparison to the Causal Plane when trying to view past lives.

This technique is a very good one. Try it tonight.

## Decompressing the File Technique

*Past-life information from the dream state may appear like a computer file compressed for document storage.*

Past-life information from the dream state may appear like a computer file compressed for document storage. The ECK Masters can impart knowledge to you by a highly compact form of communication, much like telepathy.

Now imagine turning on a computer. Slide a disk with the Master's inner discourse on it into the disk drive. Decompress the file. The computer program will do its best to honor the intent of the discourse as it converts the telepathic-like communication into everyday speech. However, no computer program can render an exact translation of an inner communication.

So catch the spirit of the message.

By all means, don't worry if your dreams don't play out as described here. The mere practice of this spiritual exercise has power. It releases the latent, invisible force that will convey a necessary past-life recall to you in some way or other.

This method is, at heart, a means to trigger past-life recall.

### An Easy Way to Resolve Karma

If you feel the burden of past-life karma in your life, here's an easy way to resolve a good part of it.

Do all deeds in the name of God or the Mahanta, the Living ECK Master. Let each task hold all your love. Even a humble chore like sweeping the kitchen floor deserves the full span of your love for the Divine Being.

*Do all deeds in the name of God or the Mahanta, the Living ECK Master. Let each task hold all your love.*

This technique brings love to the fore. An activity performed with divine love burns off karma and affords a spiritual blessing. Often, someone with a creative mind can modify this exercise and develop it as a way to Soul Travel. Listen to the Inner Master. If you have the spiritual preparation, Soul Travel allows more flexibility when exploring the higher worlds.

Do this exercise every day for a week or so. You will find life teaching you subtle ways in which to listen to the Mahanta, the Living ECK Master speak via the inner channels.

# Dreams

Why did Jim's grandmother appear in his dream?
Because of love for him.

# 6
# Spiritual View of Dreams

*O*ne morning I was up at four o'clock, and the host for a local radio station was introducing his program. Let's call him Jim. He told of a dream a short time before, which he said was profound.

Jim had been having money troubles and wondered how to resolve them. Perhaps a change of scenery would suggest an out. With that in mind, he left on a camping trip with a friend. It gave a chance to step back from the hustle and bustle of everyday living and look at himself with fresh eyes, reexamine his values, and see who and what he really was.

One night during the camping trip, Jim had a dream of his late grandmother. The dream was set in her kitchen. She handed him a catalog, pointed to it, and said, "It can solve your financial problems."

In the catalog in this dream was a circled item. It showed an Italian motorbike, a Lambretta—like the old one stored in his garage.

When Jim awoke he told his companion about the dream. Then he forgot it.

The financial impasse still loomed upon his

*Jim had a dream of his late grand-mother. The dream was set in her kitchen. She handed him a catalog, pointed to it, and said, "It can solve your financial problems."*

return home, but a windfall of two thousand dollars would resolve it.

Two months crept by. One day Jim happened to talk with another friend and spoke of the old motorbike in his garage. Though unused for years, it remained in good shape.

His friend asked, "What kind is it?"

"A Lambretta."

"What year?"

Jim told him.

His friend said, "That thing's worth two thousand dollars."

A bell rang in Jim's head. Two thousand dollars—the magic number. In that instant his dream came rushing back. So he sold the bike and was rid of his financial albatross.

That is an example of spiritual truth making its way into today's society. Why did Jim's grandmother appear in his dream? Because of love for him. So we come to the two principles: God is love, and Soul exists because God loves It.

They sum up the reason for our life and all living things.

## Wisdom from the Heart

Dreams are also a way to find wisdom from the heart. Those sincere in their search for truth—and it doesn't just mean people on the ECK path—begin to have dreams that lead to some avenue of truth. The dreams give new insights. Yet for all that, dreams are, for the most part, like seeing through a glass darkly.

People have asked me, "How are the dream teachings of Eckankar different from other dream teachings?"

*Those sincere in their search for truth—and it doesn't just mean people on the ECK path—begin to have dreams that lead to some avenue of truth.*

Dream teachings range from the silly to the highly mental. All can help one to some degree, depending upon an individual's state of consciousness. The dream teachings of ECK follow the basic pattern of all the ECK teachings: they are grounded in the physical realities as well as the spiritual (the inner, subtle side of us). So someone who wants to learn the ECK way of dreaming can study the ECK dream discourses. They are a part of membership in Eckankar.

On the other hand, a seeker can start a dream study with an ECK book on dreams, like this one. This effort opens a dreamer to the initial dream worlds of ECK, the first step to having these special dreams and understanding how they work.

*The dream teachings of ECK follow the basic pattern of all the ECK teachings: they are grounded in the physical realities as well as the spiritual (the inner, subtle side of us).*

## NAP TIME

You can begin a dream study during your naps. Anytime you feel in need of rest, set an alarm for twenty minutes. Have a notebook at hand; it will be your dream book.

Put your whole attention upon the face or presence of the Mahanta, the Living ECK Master. Do it in a light, easy, and friendly way— like meeting an old friend. Now tell yourself to enjoy a restful, peaceful nap. Remind yourself to remember some event that occurs in the dream worlds when you awaken.

Then sleep. See what comes of the experiment.

When the alarm rings, jot down all you remember, no matter how foolish or trivial. In time, your study of dreams will expand. This method of dream study is easy and causes no disruptions, even in a busy family.

Try to do it every day for two weeks. It

> takes time to learn a new skill, in dreaming as in anything else.

## Help from Dreams

A woman from Ghana we'll call Iris was scheduled for minor hand surgery. Her doctor had shown much consideration by trying to fit her into a packed schedule. It was a minor operation. Because of the general anesthetic, he cautioned, "Don't eat or drink anything before the operation."

So Iris arrived at the clinic early on the appointed morning to get on a waiting list in case of an opening in the doctor's schedule.

Iris had low blood sugar. She could only go for twelve hours without food or water without danger of collapse. Quick mental calculations when she arrived at the clinic said that since her fast began at midnight, she would last until noon. But not much longer. However, the schedule showed her operation set for 2:00 p.m. How would she manage if the doctor didn't see her by then?

Uneasy, she settled into a chair to wait.

Around 10:00 a.m., Iris began to feel ill, so she went to the nurse's office. The nurse happened to be a friend from years ago and let her rest in the nurse's office for several hours while awaiting her turn. As she rested, Iris remembered advice her sister had once given her. Her sister had said, "When it's going past your twelve hours, remember to sing HU." (It's all the names of God in one.)

So Iris began to sing HU. Soon she fell asleep and had a dream.

In this dream she held out her right hand, the one to have the operation. Someone was pouring warm tea into that hand. It felt good. She wished

*Iris remembered advice her sister had once given her. Her sister had said, "When it's going past your twelve hours, remember to sing HU."*

the feeling wouldn't stop.

A slammed door startled Iris from the dream world. When she opened her eyes, she was staring into her doctor's face.

"I'm sorry to have to tell you this," he said, "but so many emergencies have been coming in all day I won't be able to get to you until 4:00 p.m. Why don't you go out and have a couple of cups of tea—no food, just tea?" Iris thought, *This is just like my dream, where somebody was pouring warm tea on my hand and it felt so refreshing.*

Earlier, in response to her singing HU, the Mahanta, the Inner Master, had said, "Don't worry. Everything will be OK."

So she sprang from the chair, as if heading for a tennis match, and rushed from the room. The tea soon calmed her low-blood-sugar symptoms, and her body stabilized. At 4:00 p.m., the operation began.

## Bright Lights

The doctor had changed his mind. "We're just going to use a local anesthetic," he said.

So now she lay on the operating table, aware of the scalpel slicing into her hand. Then, from nowhere, a brilliant white light flooded the table. The lights in the room too surged brighter.

A startled nurse asked, "What's that?"

Doctor, nurse, and Iris all saw a white ethereal light. The doctor glanced at the ceiling, searching for the source of this dazzling light that outshone even the lights in the operating room.

Iris knew this for the Light of God. It was a sign of comfort and reassurance from the Mahanta.

After surgery, the shaken doctor said, "Your God is certainly close."

*The doctor glanced at the ceiling, searching for the source of this dazzling light that outshone even the lights in the operating room.*

A week later Iris kept an appointment for a follow-up exam in the outpatient clinic with the same doctor. He was delighted to see her. Examining her hand, he noted that the wound was healing well.

Then he asked, "What religion do you belong to?"

"Eckankar," she said.

"No wonder. I'm not surprised," he replied.

Word of Eckankar has spread to most, if not all, African countries. From the highest levels of government to the most humble of people, they know of Eckankar.

The doctor tried to rationalize what had happened during the operation on Iris. Could it have been his long working hours? Besides, he could have suffered from low blood sugar too, because he'd had trouble seeing her hand at first.

Yet as he had struggled to see, this mysterious, bright light made its appearance from nowhere. It supplied the extra light needed for a successful operation.

Iris simply thanked him for his help then said, "God is with all of us."

The heavenly light had helped the doctor, but had it helped the nurse and patient any less? The Light of God gives to all. As she left the office, Iris handed him an ECK brochure, for which he expressed much gratitude. He was open to a new spiritual direction.

*Dreams are a golden key to understanding the most secret part of ourselves.*

## Why We Dream

Dreams are a golden key to understanding the most secret part of ourselves.

Nicole, a secretary, worked at a major movie studio in California. (The names of people in this story are not their real names.) She had a reputation as a top-notch secretary, so the company moved her around like a troubleshooter and assigned her to Tony, a demanding executive. A coworker forewarned her, "Good luck. He's been through twelve secretaries in a year."

Tony was one of those overbearing people, a trial to a long-suffering staff.

Nicole had worked at this movie studio for three years and knew the ways of the company. She believed she could help Tony—protect him from his superiors and help him stay out of trouble. She understood how things were done there and was proud of her expertise.

But Tony was like a spoiled child. He flew into rages and insisted on his own way. Yet, for all that, Nicole and Tony enjoyed a fair working relationship.

A month later, the company asked Nicole to be a fill-in secretary in another department for a week. The transfer date drew near. Nicole tried to prepare Tony for her absence, keeping herself open as a clear channel for Divine Spirit. In other words, she did all in her power to ease the way for this rather impossible man.

Yet a day before Nicole was set to leave, matters reached a breaking point. Tony acted as though she didn't know her job and refused to recognize her many valuable contributions.

"This is as much as I can take," she said. Then she stormed from the room.

*Nicole tried to prepare Tony for her absence, keeping herself open as a clear channel for Divine Spirit.*

## Dream Lesson

In the past, Nicole had often had a problem dealing with such confrontations. Whenever an extreme situation arose, by reflex she'd lose her composure and overreact. Yet she knew it did spiritual harm. She determined to do better with Tony.

So Nicole returned and offered him an apology, after which they discussed their disagreement and things smoothed out.

The next day she prepared to leave for the new, weeklong assignment. Before she left, Tony said, "I would like you to come back when you finish there." She agreed to think it over and would let him know. Tony had run through twelve secretaries in a year, and after a month with him Nicole felt she'd done her time. Still, she promised to think it over.

But at her new assignment someone offered her a permanent job, an excellent career move for her. In light of the options, she jumped at the chance.

Nicole called Tony and let him know of her decision to take a new position. No, she wouldn't return. He would need to find someone else. In a feeble attempt to affirm control over her, he said, "Yes, you won't be coming back to this job." As if this were his decision.

It's an endless source of bemusement to see the lengths to which some people go to exercise control over others. To cover up his helplessness, he added, "You won't be needed." As if saying that would make a difference. Tony was thus sure to run through many more temporary secretaries, but Nicole had a new, permanent job. She was rid of him.

This entire encounter had made Nicole very curious. *What is the lesson behind this?* she wondered. What was the spiritual lesson she was supposed to have learned from this unreasonable man?

Then Nicole had a flashback.

A confrontation with Tony just before she'd left on a week's vacation came to mind. He'd been scolding her about some trifle while she stood meekly

*What is the lesson behind this? she wondered. What was the spiritual lesson she was supposed to have learned from this unreasonable man?*

before him with an icy smile. She'd recalled a passage from an ECK book: If you're ever in a bad situation, sing HU and imagine the presence of the Mahanta beside you.

So as she was receiving the onslaught of Tony's tirade, she began to sing HU and visualize the Mahanta, the Living ECK Master beside her. She continued to sing HU inside herself and felt a warm fountain of divine love flow into her heart.

Then the smile on her face, which had felt painted on, became a warm, genuine one.

Meanwhile, she watched the play of karma unwind before her like a bad movie, but it didn't bother her anymore. She could appreciate Tony as a fellow Soul. Though he was unconscious of it, Tony was helping her with her own anger and her inability to see the spiritual lesson in store for her in that face-off.

A short time after leaving Tony's employ, Nicole had a special dream. It gave a bigger picture of why she'd had to put up with him.

In this dream she was in a certain room, working on a newsletter. A lion walked in the door. He was about to spring and attack, so she shut her eyes and sang HU, again imagining the Mahanta beside her. This simple spiritual exercise turned the lion from a vicious and angry beast into a loving animal of great strength. Then it left her alone.

When Nicole awoke from this spiritual dream, she realized that her cycle of karma with Tumultuous Tony was over.

*In this dream a lion walked in the door. He was about to spring and attack, so she shut her eyes and sang HU, again imagining the Mahanta beside her.*

### DREAM BOOK

The first rule for keeping a dream book is to keep it simple. Trying to put complex scenes and ideas into words can be a daunting task. A dream may have so many details that a dreamer could well lose sight of its key points.

To overcome this potential trap, write the dream out in simple, everyday language. Then put it aside. At the end of a month, note the inner experiences that stand out from the rest. Condense these. Make believe you are an editor for *Reader's Digest.*

Then gather the best of your dream experiences and send them to the Living ECK Master in a letter. An ECK initiate may include them in an initiate report.

A dream report is an easy way to resolve karma.

## Direct Dialogue

The Mahanta, who is also the Dream Master, relies on the dream state to give spiritual instruction until a truth seeker is ready to meet him face-to-face somewhere in the heavenly worlds via Soul Travel. On the Causal Plane (the place of memories and karma), the Master uses dreams to work off karma for a chela (spiritual student). At times a dream may show a past life that has an impact on today. A filtering screen that has hidden a past-life memory lifts to give the dreamer a glimpse of that important time.

*The Dream Master may pass along health tips through dream symbols.*

Many things occur in the dream state besides giving people a spiritual education. The Dream Master may pass along health tips through dream symbols. A dreamer who is the target of psychic attacks will learn that such forms of witchcraft have power to harm only because he has somehow opened himself to them. In short, a psychic attack points out a spiritual weakness in the dreamer. The Mahanta, the Living ECK Master (the Dream Master) teaches how to shore up one's defenses and become like a mighty fortress.

So the dream state is an easy way for the Inner Master to begin teaching an individual, because it can sidestep many of a dreamer's unconscious fears.

Often when a dreamer awakens, an inner experience is still fresh. But it seems so natural and commonplace. So he forgets it.

One must therefore develop the discipline to write down in a journal, without delay, even what appears to be an insignificant dream. Read that journal entry an hour or so later, and you may be surprised at the fantastic account set down there. A dream report may prove even more surprising if it is reviewed a month or more later.

Travel is a good way to have fresh dreams. A trip to a new locale puts a traveler into a heightened state of awareness. All is new, different. At home, an alarm clock has him up at a certain hour. Cleaning up and dressing are old routines, almost automatic because of their familiarity. Then into the car and off to work. Nothing to supply dream material there. And if someone asked for a description of the third house from the corner on his street, could he do it? Probably not. The setting is too commonplace. Little in a repetitious life is apt to strike the mental screen and awaken one to dreams of a fresh and different kind.

The net result is that few people can recall their dreams.

The usual inner, or dream, state is so natural and unassuming because it blends right in. The dream life dovetails so artfully with one's daily life that

*The Mahanta, the Living ECK Master (the Dream Master) teaches how to shore up one's defenses and become like a mighty fortress.*

upon awakening a dreamer feels a dream is not worth the effort of jotting it down. By the time he's done cleaning up and dressing, every dream is gone.

So write down a few highlights to trigger a dream recall for later review.

*The gentlest technique I know is to say, "Mahanta, you have my permission to take me to a Temple of Golden Wisdom for my spiritual benefit."*

### THE GENTLEST DREAM TECHNIQUE

The gentlest technique I know is to say, "Mahanta, you have my permission to take me to a Temple of Golden Wisdom for my spiritual benefit."

As a student of ECK, I often used this technique to visit new places in the higher worlds. It works best when said at night before rest. Issue it as a thought command. Give the Inner Master permission to guide you to a celestial place that fits your state of consciousness. Then go to sleep. The next morning see if you remember even what seems to be a most humdrum event.

Daily practice will sharpen recall of the hours you spend each night outside the cramped human shell.

## Dream Protection

A young woman we'll name Patience is from an African country and has connections with the national assembly. At twenty-five, she found herself in a relationship with an older man (Victor, let's say). The relationship began with a strong mutual affection, but over time she reflected upon her future.

*Sometime I would like to marry,* she thought. *Although this man loves me very much, he's not the one I want to spend the rest of my life with because he has a very possessive love.*

Victor sensed her wish to end the relationship. He turned to black magic to prevent this. In Africa, the power of black magic is a very strong, very real force.

People in Western countries might laugh at the notion of black magic having an actual power behind it, but the Africans know better. If you ever visit Africa and a witch doctor lays a curse on you, you might find it hard to brush aside. All sorts of things may run amuck in your personal affairs unless you sing the holy word of God, HU. It serves as a shield of protection for all who chant it, for it opens hearts to protection from the Holy Spirit.

In this case, black magic had great force. Soon after Victor had it set on her, Patience began to experience nightmares. Sleep was a terrible thing. She developed a fear of sleep.

Patience happened to mention her nightmares to a friend, an ECKist. Her friend said, "You must be very careful about this practice of mysticism. It can hurt you. But there is a way to protect yourself." It was then that Patience learned of HU and how to sing it.

"Tonight when you go to bed," said her friend, "sing HU. Trust it with your whole heart. I'll sing it too, when I go to bed."

In a dream that night, Victor made advances toward her, but Patience remembered to sing HU. His advances stopped. He couldn't break through the wall of protection from Divine Spirit. In a few moments his image began to disintegrate and soon vanished from her dream.

Right after his disappearance a band of men appeared. All wore white robes but for the leader, a man in a sky blue robe.

*All sorts of things may run amuck in your personal affairs unless you sing the holy word of God, HU. It serves as a shield of protection for all who chant it, for it opens hearts to protection from the Holy Spirit.*

*Oh, oh,* she thought, *these are some of his friends; they must be black magicians who are going to try to have revenge for what's happened to him.*

To protect herself from what she took to be a new threat, Patience again began to sing HU. To her surprise, they sang along with her.

The man in blue then asked, "Where did you learn about HU?"

"From my neighbor," she replied. That was the sum of their conversation.

Early the next morning Patience knocked on her neighbor's door and told of the dream. "You've met the Mahanta," the ECKist said. "You've met the Inner Master."

Some while later Patience had a second dream. A painting of a face appeared in it. The face, painted with gold colors like an eternal face, was pleasant to behold. Yet try as she might to fix attention on this strange dream, it faded from view.

The next morning Patience returned to the home of her friend next door and told of the face painted in gold. Again came a similar reply. "You've had another dream with the Master."

Around this time her ECK friend passed along the address of the Eckankar Spiritual Center in Minneapolis. Soon thereafter, a letter from Patience crossed my desk with a request: "Please send information about ECK." She stated that HU has become her magic word. It has lent a strength and purpose to living that she never knew existed.

All live and move within the loving hands of Divine Spirit—all the time, every day, and in every place. And dream travel provides a ticket of understanding to the vast, divine creation that spans all worlds of time and space, both seen and unseen.

*Patience knocked on her neighbor's door and told of the dream. "You've met the Mahanta," the ECKist said. "You've met the Inner Master."*

## Watch Yourself Fall Asleep

At night before you retire, relax on the bed. Watch the process of falling asleep. Fix attention on a point between your eyebrows, the Spiritual Eye.

As your body relaxes and your mind settles down, a change in viewpoint occurs. The process is called falling asleep. But maintain an attitude of awareness. Notice how your body becomes quiet as your thoughts grow quiet. Hearing is often the last of the senses to leave the human consciousness. Try to catch the moment you arrive at the place between your waking and sleeping states. Be detached in this borderline state, which is like a semidream.

Then you will slip into a higher state of consciousness. Recognize it by its clarity of mental vision. It is not an unconscious state like a mental fog, but a new, more satisfying condition of awareness.

This viewpoint will last a brief moment or may stretch to several hours. With practice it could run the whole night.

To hold this lucidity, you need to walk a delicate line. Don't become too emotional or forget you are in this pre-dream state.

What is it that happens? As you put your body to rest, you (Soul) awaken in the Atma Sarup, the Soul body. You are now free to roam in the fields of eternity, beyond the shadow of death. This is part of the spiritual freedom spoken of in Eckankar.

*Watch the process of falling asleep. Fix attention on a point between your eyebrows, the Spiritual Eye.*

\* \* \*

*Listen to Beth and Dorothy tell of times a spiritual view of dreams smoothed out the stones in their paths. Both stories are from* Earth to God, Come In Please . . . , *Book 2.*

## The Secret of Graceful Living
By Beth Richards

*I began to discuss the possibility of the plan I'd dreamed about. Allowed to begin putting it into place within the company, I felt gratified at being able to follow my dreams and thanked the Inner Master, Wah Z.*

It all started with a persistent but fragmented dream. In the dream I saw myself starting a new project at work. I wrote down the dream and wondered if the program could work.

A short while later my boss and I began to discuss the possibility of the plan I'd dreamed about. Allowed to begin putting it into place within the company, I felt gratified at being able to follow my dreams and thanked the Inner Master, Wah Z.

Then my dreams took a turn. They began to warn of obstacles and discord ahead.

Several months later I took a vacation. As I relaxed, my dreams became clearer. One had a stunning message, which I recorded in my daily dream journal:

*My boss is sitting patiently but hopefully waiting for me to quit my job and leave the company. I go to her and ask if she is ready to let my coworkers know I am leaving at the beginning of the month.*

*As I speak to her, a wave of anxiety comes over me. I do not have another job lined up. How will I cover the mortgage on my house? Then a voice tells me I am experiencing fear. "There is no room for fear," the voice says. I start jumping for joy, realizing I am going to my next step in life.*

When I awoke, I felt confused. I had followed my earlier dreams and started a new program at work, but no one else in the company knew the details of the project to assume the task. If Divine Spirit did not want me to work at the company, why had It directed me to implement this complicated program?

Were my dreams true? How could I let my boss down when she had trusted me so much?

And more important, where would I go without a job—especially since the beginning of the month was only one week away? I felt foolish and unstable.

I decided to wait and take no action. Let the dream manifest in the awakened, outer arena of life. Meanwhile, I kept my eyes open for clues. Slowly, conflict arose at work. Several confrontations with a powerful administrative committee led to one officer saying, "We may need to eventually get rid of you, if you don't cooperate."

From that moment on, I felt under attack by various people in the company. Even my boss became an unconscious adversary, under the influence of others.

Five months later, the situation was intolerable. My dreams were coming true. I realized Divine Spirit was telling me: You are no longer needed at this particular job. Your presence is unbalancing here. So I gathered my courage and stepped into my boss's office. We discussed the situation. Then I took a chance and told her about my dreams, before quietly resigning.

My boss, stunned by my revelations, said, "You're very perceptive, Beth. I can't say too much more, just that you're right about needing to move on."

Then she continued in a more thoughtful vein, "I don't know why, but I have always really liked you. I can't put my finger on why that is, or why others in the company are opposed to you." We

*I realized Divine Spirit was telling me: You are no longer needed at this particular job.*

agreed I would leave as soon as they found a replacement. I promised to make the transition as comfortable as possible for the company.

From that moment, my boss and I became closer.

But weeks passed and neither the company nor I seemed able to part, and I was having real trouble finding a new job. Everyone seemed to procrastinate in finding a replacement for me. Problems arose in every direction with the clients I was serving, delaying my departure.

Various people in the company seemed to want me to stay. But no one would say anything. It was as if they were waiting for me to change my mind. I had a difficult time reconciling the idea of being forced, on the inner and the outer, out of a job I loved, with clients I had faithfully served. My decision to leave my comfortable, tailor-made job seemed quite irrational.

Was I heading for disaster?

Others had been forced out of the company just like me, and clients had suffered unjust abuses. Shouldn't I stand up for my rights and help put a stop to this kind of behavior? Every time doubt set in, anger and resentment would creep into my heart.

*Each day, I contemplated on the situation. The answer and feeling I always got was, "Leave!"*

I consulted several lawyers to see what recourse was available. Doors closed one by one, and I really did not want to pursue litigation. It was too financially and emotionally draining.

Meanwhile, a persistent image of "jumping for joy at my next step in life" had taken residence in my mind.

Each day, I contemplated on the situation. The answer and feeling I always got was, "Leave!"

Not too subtle. I decided a peaceful resolution was the only answer, despite my misgivings and anger. I needed to trust that the ECK always works in my best interest. My dreams had seldom failed me before.

I finally set a deadline. In two months I would leave the company, even though I was still uncertain about my future. This was truly a test of faith.

My boss gave a nice letter of recommendation at my request. In turn, I wrote her a personal letter of gratitude for the opportunity to serve, and included two Eckankar books with my letter. She was delighted!

My attitude changed, and I began to pour love into the entire situation. I cleaned and organized everything in my office. Every loose end was tied up. I made peace and chatted amicably with two staff members who had had repeated conflicts with me.

*Exactly two weeks after quitting, I found a new job. I am entering my next step with such joy and satisfaction!*

When the time came, I left as quietly and inconspicuously as possible. The company unexpectedly gave me two weeks of severance pay.

Exactly two weeks after quitting, I found a new job. I am entering my next step with such joy and satisfaction! Now I have an inkling of what Sri Harold Klemp meant when he said we must live gracefully in accord with Divine Spirit.

## Dream Healing
By Dorothy Thomas

My family was grieving over three deaths in short order. Then, on New Year's Eve, my brother died a tragic, sudden death. How could I cope with another loss?

On the eve of my brother's funeral, I asked the Inner Master to give me strength in the days ahead. That night in a dream I met my brother in a large white ballroom. We waltzed while the Dream Master looked on.

The next morning I felt calm and peace within. It reassured me of my strength to face my brother's funeral with confidence and courage.

After the funeral I postponed my return trip and sent my family on ahead. I wanted to spend time with my mother. We had all pitched in two days before to help her dispose of my brother's belongings, but there were a few remaining items.

As my mother and I sorted through them, Mom's grief soared. It almost overwhelmed me. As I tried to comfort her, my thoughts went back to my dream. How could I tell her my brother was fine? That there was no cause to be concerned, for he was happy?

Suddenly she stopped weeping. She walked into my brother's room, sat down, and put her head in her hands. I sat quietly beside her, feeling powerless and inadequate.

When she finally looked up at me, her words of bewilderment told me she'd forgotten what had transpired in the past few days. I slowly talked to her about the events of the tragedy, and she nodded in recognition. But something had just occurred here beyond what I could see or understand, so I asked her to tell what she had seen or felt.

*To my amazement, my mother confided that just moments ago she'd had a vision. It was so vivid.*

To my amazement, my mother confided that just moments ago she'd had a vision. It was so vivid. It had banished all sense of time and physical reality.

"I saw your father and several other deceased relatives," she said. "They were celebrating joyfully. I also heard your brother's voice join in with them, even though I couldn't see him."

"Then he spoke to me!"

As I listened and watched her acknowledge the reality of her experience, her face softened. A peaceful calm swept over her. I knew the Inner Master had helped not only me but my loved ones deal with my brother's death.

One evening before sleep, she did a visualization technique. It was to imagine herself in a place of healing.

# 7
# Dream Travel: Doorway to Your Inner Worlds

*L*yn (not her real name) was studying dreams. One night, in a dream, the Mahanta (Dream Master) gave her two phone numbers. The only clues from him were these: one was for a home phone, and the other was an office number.

When Lyn awoke, she remembered the dream. But should she call these two numbers? How do you tell someone on the other end, "I just had a dream, and God told me to call you"?

This dream is reminiscent of a Gary Larson *Far Side* cartoon, in which Larson displays an acute insight into human nature. In this cartoon a phone rings, and a man picks up the receiver. A voice says, "Hello, this is God." The man asks who God wants. God gives a name. The man says he is sorry, but God has a wrong number.

The caption underneath the cartoon reads: After that, he never stopped telling people that he had talked to God.

But Lyn's story takes a different turn. About a month after her dream, Lyn called the first number and got an answering machine. She left a message, "Please call me when you can. I got your number,

*How do you tell someone on the other end, "I just had a dream, and God told me to call you"?*

and I would like to make a connection here." Then she called the second number and left a similar message on that answering machine too.

The next day she received a call from a woman, who said, "I got your phone message. What is it exactly that you want to know?"

"I had this dream," said Lyn. "In the dream I got your phone number. Is there any connection that you might make from this?" The other replied, "Could you tell me a little about yourself?" Lyn said, "Well, I live in Texas and have raised four children. I was a social worker." She further mentioned the loss of a son, who took his life in his twenties.

The woman replied, "It just so happens that I was a dream consultant."

She used to live and work in another state. There, she'd had her own radio program, gave interviews, and talked with people about their dreams. Therefore, it was most unusual to hear from someone who got her phone number in a dream.

*As the conversation went on, the dream consultant asked, "What exactly do you want to know?"*

*Lyn said, "I want to know if there was any karma on my part that caused my son's suicide."*

As the conversation went on, the dream consultant asked, "What exactly do you want to know?"

Lyn said, "I want to know if there was any karma on my part that caused my son's suicide."

The dream consultant replied, "When you're ready, you will get an answer."

But Lyn wanted an answer right then. Why else would the Dream Master have given her the phone number of this woman who turned out to have been a dream consultant?

The consultant explained. When she used to give advice on her radio show, some people called back because they felt she hadn't given a clear, direct interpretation of their dreams. So she simply told them, "When you're ready, you will get the answer."

But these people were impatient and often grew angry. They wanted answers right then.

Lyn understood. She said, "I understand it's my responsibility. When I'm ready, I will get my answer. I also understand that my son's suicide is entirely his responsibility."

She had been afraid to go to sleep at night because of a fear that the Inner Master might reveal the answer before she was ready for it. Yet the dream consultant's answer was an assurance. Lyn had only to wait. When the time was right—in a week, a month, ten years, whatever it took—she would get her answer.

Lyn asked a final question of the dream consultant, "Where can I find your books? Will they be in a regular bookstore?"

"Actually, this is the most unusual way that Divine Spirit has ever had someone contact me," the other said, "so I'll send you the books."

Thus from this first phone contact, Lyn understood she was not responsible for her son's suicide. She further received the assurance of finding the answer for any karmic involvement in the right time and season. An additional insight from the dream consultant was this: "His suicide affected many people. And if I gave you a direct answer right now, what would you do with it? Would you carry the answer to some people who are not ready for it yet?"

And the dream consultant added: "The dream worlds are the real worlds. This world is the dream."

And so ended the first phone call.

The second day Lyn received another call. It was from a sales professional. Again Lyn explained, "I had this dream, and I got your number."

*The dream consultant added: "The dream worlds are the real worlds. This world is the dream."*

"I don't want to be rude," the caller said, "but I want to remind you this is a long-distance call."

"May I call you back?" Lyn asked. He agreed. Again she told about the death of her son and explained the unusual way she'd received the salesman's number. "Can you make a connection of any sort in this?" Lyn asked.

In a very matter-of-fact voice he said, "Three people died in my family recently. People die."

After a bit more conversation, he said, "This is all I can do to help you. I think I've been very fair to you." Lyn agreed. He'd been very generous in giving of his time to a total stranger.

After the conversation came to an end, Lyn realized that Divine Spirit had given a spiritual message through him too. She gleaned the importance of (1) being a bit more careful about financial matters (the expense of the long-distance call), and (2) not becoming so attached to material things, including her loved ones.

Lyn had been seeking an answer to her karmic involvement with her son's suicide. So the Master spoke to her through two human agents of the Holy Spirit whom she could relate to.

*Whenever you carry out some act of service for the ECK with love, it is because of the love for the Sound and Light of God that fills you.*

## SEMINAR DREAMS

Sometimes you find yourself on the inner planes in settings very much like an Eckankar seminar. Maybe you serve as an usher there or play some other important role.

Whenever you carry out some act of service for the ECK with love, it is because of the love for the Sound and Light of God that fills you.

Do you wish to attend an Eckankar seminar on the inner planes? Then try the following technique.

Before sleep go into contemplation. Visualize every possible detail you can about the seminar site. For guidance, read the description in the latest preregistration brochure from Eckankar for the upcoming ECK seminar. Then imagine yourself at it on the inner planes.

Now say, "I see myself with friends at this ECK seminar. I see myself in the audience, listening to the Master."

If you wish to be conscious of giving love through service as an usher or some other duty, say this two-part silent command before sleep. Then let the matter rest. It is in the hands of Spirit.

See what comes.

## God Speaks to Us

There are a number of ways God communicates with people.

God may speak directly through the divine Sound or Light. Sometimes in contemplation or during the day you'll see a blue or white light. Know this for the presence of God. It's the presence of God come to uplift you in spirit, to purify your heart, to prepare you for the next leg of your journey into the heart of God's full love and mercy.

On other occasions, God may speak through the holy Sound alone, like the sound of a musical instrument. You will hear a single instrument or a number of them playing some celestial delight.

Again, God may choose to speak with the rumble of a storm or in the peal of thunder. Others have reported a distant drum. Or a birdsong. Sometimes the air may only quiver with the breath of a soft sigh.

*Sometimes in contemplation or during the day you'll see a blue or white light. Know this for the presence of God.*

*If it leaves you feeling light, joyful, or uplifted, filled with goodness and love, then be assured that the sound was God's blessing in one of many voices.*

Expect almost any sound at all. If it leaves you feeling light, joyful, or uplifted, filled with goodness and love, then be assured that the sound was God's blessing in one of many voices.

A Voice of God came to bless you.

A more usual way for God to speak is through dreams. But dreams are more indirect. Because they often employ symbols, any interpretation of them takes some care. It's like seeing through a dark cloud.

Then a dreamer must learn the rudiments of dream interpretation.

Your experiences in the higher worlds are clouded by illusion. Things are not as they seem. The negative power we call the Kal (some know it as Satan or the devil) has a divine mission too. His purpose is to trick and mislead a dreamer and make him miss the point of a dream. This negative force wants you to say dreams aren't important.

Once an individual is no longer fooled by the devilment of the Kal, that Soul has seen through some illusions and so gains in spiritual love and power.

I say dreams are important. They are one way God speaks right to you.

## Dream Journal

Robert from Nigeria became a member of Eckankar. (All names in this story are changed to protect privacy.) After Robert had studied the ECK teachings for two years, he received the Second Initiation. This simple rite lifts one to the Astral (emotions) Plane, the next level above this physical one.

He journeyed to a far city to attend an ECK

seminar, and when it ended he caught a ride halfway back to his home city with other ECKists. At the midway point, he planned to catch a cab for the rest of the journey. So he bade his friends farewell and made his way to a cabstand. Because it was a long distance to Robert's hometown, a cabdriver liked to wait until his cab was full. Robert was lucky. He was the last passenger. The vehicle was loaded, ready to roll.

But then, trouble. When Robert reached for his wallet to make sure he could pay at his destination, he was shocked by a terrible discovery: his wallet was missing. He flew into a panic.

He pleaded with the cabbie, "Take me to my hometown, and I'll pay you there."

The cabbie had heard that one before. Should he trust this guy? Such a long trip. As the cabdriver chewed the situation over in his mind, Robert felt more and more distress—no wallet, no money, no keys, no ECK ID card. How would he reach home?

Then one of the other passengers broke the impasse. "That's OK," he said. "I'll pay his fare." Robert thanked his benefactor and promised, "I'll pay you as soon as we get to my hometown."

The other replied, "It's not necessary."

From this act of generosity, Robert got the feeling that the Mahanta, the Living ECK Master had a message for him in this experience. The spiritual leader of ECK was trying to teach him some important lesson. So Robert ran up his spiritual antenna, trying to determine what it could be.

Upon reaching home, he tried to repay his benefactor. But it was Sunday. The banks were closed, so he couldn't obtain the means. As he debated his next move, someone came to the front door of his

*Robert got the feeling that the Mahanta, the Living ECK Master had a message for him in this experience.*

home. This fellow was a representative of a former client, for whom Robert had once done consulting work. The stranger handed him a large sum of cash. Now there was plenty of money to reimburse his angel for the cab ride.

The matter of cab fare was thus resolved to the satisfaction of all.

But Robert faced a problem apart from the missing wallet. He'd also lost his keys. A teacher at a large university, he needed them to enter his office. Worse, the lost keys were the only set. Robert seldom took them on trips, but this time he'd forgotten. So now he was locked out of his office. What to do?

*That night in a dream the Inner Master appeared and spoke to him.*

*"What about your dream journal?"* the Dream Master asked.

That night in a dream the Inner Master appeared and spoke to him.

"What about your dream journal?" the Dream Master asked.

Robert searched his memory. "I did buy a notebook and was going to start recording my dreams right after the Second Initiation," he said. "But I forgot."

He'd had good dream experiences. In one, he now remembered the Dream Master's warning about some people who planned to start a business venture with him but were of a dishonest sort. He'd heeded the warning and was able to protect himself. It saved him a lot of money. Robert could have recorded that case in his dream journal, but he'd neglected to do so.

The Master asked, "What about your initiate report? Where is this report you should be writing for your own benefit each month? Even if you don't mail it, just write it."

"I forgot," said Robert. He was becoming aware

of the utter neglect of his spiritual disciplines.

The Master used an illuminating term to describe his failing: "Indiscipline." Not "lack of discipline," but "indiscipline."

"The lost wallet and keys are a waking dream of locking yourself out of the spiritual worlds by indiscipline," the Inner Master said. "You have to make changes if you want to open up your spiritual life."

Before long, Robert had a second dream. In it, he met a friend from the same city that was the site of the ECK seminar he'd attended.

"I found your wallet," said his friend. "I'll send it to you with a note."

But the next morning Robert felt misgivings about the dream. So when an acquaintance from home told of plans to visit that city, Robert entrusted him with a note to his friend about the dream. "If you find my wallet," he wrote, "please send it back."

The next day his wallet arrived. The keys and his ECK ID were intact, so everything was back in order.

Upon reflection, Robert knew that his wallet was never lost at all. It was just in someone else's care. He realized that this whole situation was a gift from the Master to help him with spiritual disciplines. It was an act of grace from God to speed him on his journey home.

*He realized that this whole situation was a gift from the Master to help him with spiritual disciplines. It was an act of grace from God to speed him on his journey home.*

## Karma in Dreams

Karma may also work off in the dream state or in some other way.

For example, people have car accidents in the dream state instead of having such a purifying, though upsetting, event in everyday life. Still others have the actual accident, but a miracle turns aside serious injury or worse. No one claims that the teachings of ECK are a panacea for all ills. Far from it. This life is about meeting ourselves.

*This life is about meeting ourselves.*

That said, more challenging things do come to light that one must face—not only to pay off past debts, but also to grow in spiritual stature.

The play of karma is at the root of all human relationships.

In this next story a young man has to balance the scales of justice from past karma. He needs to repay a victim from a previous life. Yet the Mahanta, the Living ECK Master (the spiritual leader of Eckankar) sends a dream to prepare him for the necessary, yet painful, experience to come.

Nick, we'll say, told of a dream in which a beautiful young woman arrived at his office. She wanted to use the phone on his manager's desk. Nick and the girl felt an immediate attraction for each other, and a passionate romance soon evolved. But to his frustration it led nowhere.

Then he awoke.

Weeks later, a young female student began a stint at the office to gain work experience. Nick loved her from the start. He did everything in his power to win her heart, but she played coy and brushed aside his passion with promises. Later, always later. Soon everyone in the office was abuzz with talk of their relationship.

Then the sky fell in.

Via the office grapevine Nick learned of the secret love affair between her and his best friend at work. It had begun the first week of her arrival. Worse, Nick had set the stage. That first week required him to work late one night, so he asked his good friend to see her home. It was the beginning of the end.

Only the ECK, Divine Spirit, kept Nick from losing his mind when he learned of the secret love affair. But he did turn sour on life. Why had this beautiful young woman come—to bring grief?

In his anxiety and anger, he forgot the spiritual love of the Mahanta, the Living ECK Master.

Then, a second dream. The Mahanta took him on the Time Track and showed him a past life in which he was a woman. Married to a wealthy man, this individual (Nick, now) had two house servants, both of whom suffered due to Nick's abuse of position and authority. One was this student.

"You made that karma," the Mahanta explained. "That debt stands between you and God's love. Pay now and be done with it."

In the end, Nick recognized the hand of karma and the long, outstanding debt that he needed to settle. It took a while for the crushing pain to subside, of course, but now he's happy the debt is paid. After the pain was gone, there came a new sense of freedom and lightness. God's love could now shine directly into his heart.

The obstructing block of karmic debt had vanished.

## Changing Destiny

A little-known benefit of a true Master is his ability to change fate. He has the spiritual power to alter the line of destiny once an individual reaches a higher state of consciousness. If there is enough unfoldment, a true Master will cancel unnecessary karma.

*A little-known benefit of a true Master is his ability to change fate.*

It is off the books.

Often karma clears up in the dream state. In this case, one who needs a certain experience may get it in a dream. Next morning the dreamer says, "What a dream! Sure hope it doesn't happen here."

It needn't; it has run its course. The individual has paid the piper in that dream for whatever was owed.

This consideration is a gift from the Master.

Some years ago doctors told Rebecca she was barren—never to bear her own children. A member of Eckankar, she believes in dreams. Despite this gloomy forecast by doctors, she still felt a strong desire to be a natural mother, to bring forth children of her own. So she opened her heart to Divine Spirit.

She said, "If there's a way for me to have my own children, please let it be so."

She then determined to live her religion. As an ECKist, she began to do the spiritual exercises every day. Rebecca read ECK books. She practiced the ECK principles to the best of her ability.

Rebecca, by such means, was spiritualizing her state of consciousness.

She put the best possible light on everything in her life to uplift herself, because she knew that the power of God can then get to the heart.

One evening before sleep, she did a visualization technique. It was to imagine herself in a place of healing. Later, in a dream, she was in a large hospital in some other world where a doctor did an exam, then wheeled her into an operating room to perform surgery. After the operation, he handed her a prescription. It listed the name of a medication, which she memorized.

*Often karma clears up in the dream state.*

The moment he mentioned its name, she felt a definite movement in her lower abdomen. Something was stirring. Then she awoke.

Rebecca recorded the dream in her diary. On a separate piece of paper she jotted the name of the medication, then fell back to sleep.

The next morning, she called several pharmacies to locate the dream drug. Everywhere the answer was the same. "Madame, this drug is very rare; you can only get it at the regional hospitals and some big, private clinics." It was a new drug.

Rebecca considered her options. She thought, *I can't really go to a doctor and say, 'Here's my dream prescription. Would you fill it, please?'* She decided to let the matter rest.

She'd wait for God's own time.

Rebecca went about her life and, for the most part, forgot this dream. Then one morning she awoke with a terrible toothache. Her gums were swollen. It felt as if her teeth would fall out. Her supervisor at work gave her leave to seek relief at a dental clinic.

Upon her arrival, a dentist took a look at the painful tooth. "You've got quite an infection here," he said. "I'm going to write you a prescription." He told the name of the medication—the very same remedy the doctor in her dream had prescribed. It was the rare, new wonder drug.

Rebecca returned home with the prescription. And before the bottle was empty, she was delighted to find herself pregnant. The child, to date, was seven years of age.

This child was her proof of the Mahanta's presence, that he is always with her. He'd heard her heartfelt request.

*This child was her proof of the Mahanta's presence, that he is always with her. He'd heard her heartfelt request.*

Dreams are thus another way to receive answers from the Holy Spirit.

\* \* \*

*These four personal accounts tell about the power of dreams. They are pure gold. They appeared in* Earth to God, Come In Please . . . , *Books 1 and 2.*

### Setting Myself Free
By Larry White

Night after night I had the same nightmare. A man with a knife chased me.

It didn't matter where I was or whom I was with in the dream, he would pop out of nowhere and chase me. Around corners, down unlit streets and alleys, through abandoned buildings, he was always in pursuit.

To make things even less pleasant, the faster I tried to run, the slower my legs would go. It was like trying to sprint underwater. My legs grew heavier, and just before capture I awoke in a cold sweat.

My line of work demands an alert state of mind. The want of sleep was a threat to my job security, leading my boss to ask whether I held a second job. He felt I was sleepwalking through the days.

I decided to end this dream madness.

The next time this stranger pursued me in the dream state, I determined to turn around and demand, "What do you want from me?" After all, the Living ECK Master has emphasized how much one can learn from dreams. Confronting a dream situation face-to-face is better than running from it: a reminder to myself.

That night I lay in bed, ready for action. I

*The next time this stranger pursued me in the dream state, I determined to turn around and demand, "What do you want from me?"*

repeated to myself, "Tonight I am going to confront the man with the knife. Tonight I am going to ask him what he wants from me."

Eventually, I slipped into repose. In no time I woke refreshed from a full night's rest—but without the recall of a single dream.

It was a better day at work than usual.

That night I repeated my inner directive to confront the man in my dreams. Again nothing came of it. Was this good? Was getting rid of one silly nightmare worth wiping out all my other dreams? My boss didn't care; he was happy to have his employee back full-time.

The third night I repeated the postulate. But I felt more detached.

All of a sudden I awoke in the dream state, flipping through albums in a record store. My search was for one particular album. What did it look like? No idea. However, I had every confidence of recognizing it once my fingers touched it.

About to give up and leave, I spotted the desired album on a wall rack. Its name was *Look at Yourself.* The cover was an actual mirror, and it was a strange feeling to see my reflection staring back at me: a very sad face indeed.

The reflection held yet another image: a man screaming, "You'll never amount to anything!"

It was the awful man with the knife.

I took off at a fast run out of the store, then on through the mall. The familiar footsteps pounded hot on my trail. The faster I tried to run, the slower my legs would churn. An instant later, I remembered my resolve to confront this mysterious stranger. So I stopped dead in my tracks and spun around.

*I remembered my resolve to confront this mysterious stranger. So I stopped dead in my tracks and spun around.*

"What do you want from me?" I demanded. "Thank God," the panting man said. "I thought you'd never stop running away."

Shutting my eyes to await the worst, I was startled to hear an odd grating sound. My eyes snapped open. The man, crouched at my feet, was using the knife like a saw to cut a ball and chain from each of my legs, to set them free. Then, with compassion on his face, he said, "You've got to stop blackballing yourself. There. Now you're free."

I awoke and recorded the dream. The realization struck how I'd been holding myself back. There was an opening for a much better job at another company that I hadn't felt worthy to apply for, so the opportunity came to nothing.

Echoes from my past included "You'll never amount to anything." It was a message oft repeated and set into old, well-established grooves of thought. This recording played over and over.

But was that a reason to keep sabotaging my life?

The next day after work I drew up a list of all my job skills. Upon finishing it, I was surprised at the breadth of experience. The next step was to create a résumé from the list and submit it to the other company. They called me in for an interview that morning.

The company hired me on the spot.

Since this dream experience I have released many old recordings of fear and replaced them with the unconditional love of ECK. Whether hideous or beautiful, my dreams have been blessings full of truth.

*Since this dream experience I have released many old recordings of fear and replaced them with the unconditional love of ECK.*

## Inner Contract

By E. K. Tyrrell

Several years ago I had a vivid dream whose meaning eluded me for months.

In it, I found myself in a small study or library. A High Initiate of ECK stood behind the desk. We'd never met in the waking life, but I had often enjoyed her many talks and workshops at Eckankar seminars.

Now her smile was full of love. She slid a paper across the desk for me to sign. As I wrote my name on the dotted line, I felt yet another presence in the room. There stood Wah Z, the inner form of the Living ECK Master, at the other end of the desk, in white shirt and trousers.

Wah Z gathered up a sheaf of contracts like the one I'd signed. He did not look at me or speak. After collecting the papers, he slipped from the room. Upon awakening, I felt that something of great importance was about to happen.

I later wrote to the High Initiate in my dream and described in detail the small study and my inner experience there. Within a short time came her reply.

The letter confirmed my description of the study in her own home.

She expressed gratitude that the Mahanta had chosen her as a channel for ECK and suggested the dream might mean I should strive to be all I could be. In reference to the contract, she said the interpretation of what it meant should be mine and mine alone.

Yet there was more to learn from this dream.

*I felt yet another presence in the room. There stood Wah Z, the inner form of the Living ECK Master, at the other end of the desk, in white shirt and trousers.*

Next, I researched all the Eckankar books for references to inner contracts, but nothing turned up. So I gave up the search.

Not long after, my husband of forty-five years (also an ECKist) was diagnosed with a terminal illness. We went through a long, dark period of testing and spiritual growth as we prepared to say good-bye.

Our Eckankar friends lent love and constant help. No task was too great or too small, and they offered assistance before it was asked. One High Initiate, a nurse, came from work almost every night to give me a rest from taking care of my husband.

Another ECKist, also a nurse, did everything to make him comfortable both at home and in the hospital. She helped my family and me cope with the stress.

After my husband's translation (passing) to another plane of existence, there was a memorial service in our home. The High Initiate who conducted it did so with much love and humility. My husband's family, though not ECKists, gained much comfort from it and remarked over and over on the beauty of the service.

Several days after his passing, my husband appeared to me at home. He seemed as real as you or me, as he sat with me in our favorite spot on the couch. He looked so well, so strong and healthy. I could not believe my eyes.

All of a sudden, he looked me straight in the eye.

"Do you want to come with me now," he asked, "or finish your contract?"

After having loved him for four-and-a-half

*Several days after his passing, my husband appeared to me at home. He seemed as real as you or me, as he sat with me in our favorite spot on the couch.*

decades the pull to go was great, but somehow I knew we had learned as much as we could together. Now it was time to go separate ways, for each would progress faster on our own. I would finish my contract of service.

Two years have passed since his death. In the meantime I learned many lessons about self-responsibility and self-discipline. Of course, there were still times of loneliness and doubt.

One very bad night I cried out, "What is this all about?"

In desperation I opened *The Shariyat-Ki-Sugmad*, Book One. These are the scriptures of ECK.

My eyes fell on the words: "Whether the chela [student] is living on the Physical Plane or the Atma Lok [Soul Plane], he never feels he is in a separate world, or state. . . . He does not feel like either a citizen or an alien, but rather like a modern traveler who goes through each country as a tourist or for business.

"The entities of each plane look upon their existence there as sort of a contract of service."

And further down the page: "Servitude on earth in the human form, or in any of the psychic planes, is a small price to pay if it purchases a ticket to the true Kingdom of God, which is by the way of Eckankar."

I had completed the cycle. Here was the answer to all my questions, the answer to my dream. I'd come full circle. I found that the joy that comes from true service to God banishes, in the end, all fears and doubts for the Soul traveling home to God.

*I found that the joy that comes from true service to God banishes, in the end, all fears and doubts for the Soul traveling home to God.*

## Escape from the Pit
By Ed Adler

Eckankar is a spiritual teaching that shows one the way back home to God. For me, that journey began with a mysterious dream a few weeks after I had applied for membership in Eckankar.

"Somebody help me—please!" I cried in this dream.

The stench around me was unbearable. Up to my waist in a steamy, foul-smelling cesspool of mud, I was horrified of sinking even deeper. Nausea beat through me in endless waves. I struggled to get free of the mess which held me with clawlike fingers.

*Could this be hell?* I wondered.

If it was, it was much worse than I'd ever imagined. Never had I felt so helpless.

I struggled to the point of exhaustion, then stopped to figure out where I was. At first there was nothing but my fear and the darkness. By the light of a dim reflection from above, it was possible to make out a cavernous space that rose hundreds of feet above me. Somehow I knew I was trapped in the basement of a tall building.

As I looked around for help, I saw someone against the far wall, near a bank of brightly lit elevators. He was a tall, slim, ebony-skinned young man with a warm smile. However, his piercing black eyes gazed right through me.

"Why don't you help me?" I shouted.

He answered by unfolding his arms and beckoning me to come toward him.

*What's this?* I thought. *He wants me to get over there by myself. But that's impossible! I'm really stuck.*

*Eckankar is a spiritual teaching that shows one the way back home to God. For me, that journey began with a mysterious dream.*

Yet there was nothing to lose by trying. What is amazing, I found the strength to fight through the sludge to where he stood. He reached down to help me up and out. I was free at last, at least from the noisome pit, but little did I know that my adventure had just begun.

He didn't say a word but simply pointed to one of the waiting elevators.

It was the strangest-looking device I'd ever seen. There were no sides or top, just a plain wooden platform with an upright control lever. Stepping on the platform, he nodded for me to follow. Full of doubt I walked to the strange contraption and stepped on too, then noticed a young lady standing nearby. Who knows where she came from. Without a word she joined us on the elevator.

*Who is she?* I wondered.

I strained to see her face but inexplicably couldn't focus my eyes. Her features remained a blur. (It would be several years before I discovered her identity.)

Meanwhile, the silent young man pushed down on the control lever, and we flew up with amazing speed. In my waking life I suffered from an uncontrollable fear of heights and was now terrified to look down at the fast-disappearing basement floor.

With great effort I forced my eyes from the dizzying space below to the serene face of our guide. My icy fear melted in the warmth of his quiet assurance. The mystery woman also showed no concern about our swift ascent, and I relaxed a little.

Despite our great speed we climbed a long time, higher and higher. Finally we reached the

*With great effort I forced my eyes from the dizzying space below to the serene face of our guide.*

*When the golden-white light exploded through the heavy sky, there was no sense of time. Every square inch of creation bathed in the loving light of truth.*

top and stepped with care onto a flat gray gravel roof. The atmosphere was gray too. And the heavy mist was an oppressive blanket that allowed barely enough light to see the next step. As we groped to the edge of the roof, I was aware of a deep abyss only one step away. How I wished for more light. Every cell in my body cried for more light!

Without warning, our guide raised an arm. He pointed to a spot in the blind gray sky where, from behind the leaden veil, he inferred the brilliant sun would soon be shining. He kept pointing.

How long we stood there I'm not sure. It could have been a split second or a thousand years. When the golden-white light exploded through the heavy sky, there was no sense of time. Every square inch of creation bathed in the loving light of truth. There was no more fear, pain, anger, jealousy, hate, despair, or loneliness anywhere—nor boundaries or separation! All things had their being in the One.

What was there to seek? All there ever was or would be existed in the here and now.

How I yearned to remain in that glorious moment forever, but the beautiful vision melted away. It was morning, and I was sitting on my bed at home. Tears of joy and wonder flooded down my cheeks.

*Has this all been just a wild dream?* I asked myself.

"No, of course not!"

The instant response had come from within my heart. I knew this experience was a precious gift that would change me forever.

\* \* \*

The next day, a letter arrived with an invitation to a local Eckankar Satsang, or study class. It filled me with joy and anticipation. Somehow, I knew it had everything to do with my dream. The warm letter from the Arahata (teacher) informed me that the class was to meet in a few days.

On a brisk January evening three nights later, I walked up to a large apartment house in a fine, old residential district of the city. I knocked on the front door, my hands trembling from more than just the chill wind. Already, a giant wave of joy flowed through the solid oak door. I hesitated a moment, frozen with the sudden realization that once the door opened, my life would never be the same. I shook myself and knocked once more—boldly this time, in an attempt to conquer my lingering fears.

The door opened wide. A tall, slim ebony-skinned college student with a warm smile and piercing black eyes greeted me.

"Can I help you?" he asked.

My voice shook, but I managed to choke out, "Thanks, you already have!"

"Hi, I'm Al," he said in a quiet tone and invited me in.

It was hard to look at Al in class that evening. The golden-white light dancing around his head and shoulders was so dazzling and brilliant that it brought burning tears to my eyes.

*If this is what it's like to be with a teacher of Eckankar,* I thought, *what will it be like when I meet the Master?*

It was an exciting and dynamic time of discovery and change for our small Satsang class as we explored new inner and outer worlds each

*The golden-white light dancing around his head and shoulders was so dazzling and brilliant that it brought burning tears to my eyes.*

meeting. Al was a firm but gentle teacher, and miracles were becoming a commonplace for each of us. Bit by bit our class increased in size over those early months, and strangers became loving family in no time at all.

When Marie joined us, there was something about her that made me wonder if we had met before.

She was an attractive, fair-haired young woman with blue eyes that seemed to see into the deep mysteries of Spirit. As we continued our studies I often thought to ask if we had met before, but little by little the idea faded from my mind.

Sometime later, a small group of us were traveling to an Eckankar workshop. The conversation shifted from the beautiful weather to an exciting discussion of our inner adventures. I was just beginning to describe my adventure in the cesspool when Marie stopped me.

*Satsang is a vital channel—a way for Spirit to encourage and guide each Soul on the long journey back home to God.*

"Don't you know who the other passenger on the elevator was?"

I must have responded with a blank expression, because she continued, "That was me!"

Then she described with surprising accuracy every single detail—from the wild elevator ride to the golden-white light bursting through the heavy gray mist.

This story may seem like science fiction to some, but it is just one of the many spiritual adventures shared by members of my local Eckankar Satsang class during the time we studied together. Where are the words to express our joy, gratitude, and wonder?

Satsang is a vital channel—a way for Spirit to encourage and guide each Soul on the long journey back home to God.

## Kicking the Cigarette Habit

By John London

Shortly before an Eckankar seminar in Orlando, Florida, I recorded this dream about my smoking habit in my dream journal: *I was parked in my pickup truck, smoking a cigarette. I kept dropping it in my lap, on the floor, on the steering column.*

At the seminar, every time I turned a corner, stopped at a light, or bent over in my car, I dropped my cigarette, just as in my dream. The ECK was telling me it was time to drop the cigarette habit.

But sometimes it's not easy to quit a long-held habit. One day while walking to my office, I asked the Mahanta out loud, "Is smoking really that bad? What effect is it having on me spiritually?" What drawbacks could there be to smoking?

No answer came to settle my question that minute, so I was quick to forget about it. But the Inner Master didn't.

That night I had another dream. I was sitting on the patio when a friend and his young son walked up. "Come with us," my friend said.

They led me around the side of the house. Cigarette butts, old crumpled packs, and empty cartons covered the yard. What a mess! We got busy and filled the trash can to overflowing. And there was still more trash to pick up as the dream faded.

This time I listened hard. I knew the Master had answered my question. He had shown what effect smoking was having on me: it was trashing my consciousness! Success with the Spiritual Exercises of ECK and smoking are not compatible.

*I knew the Master had answered my question. He had shown what effect smoking was having on me: it was trashing my consciousness!*

Cigarette smoke clouds one's inner vision. As a new ECKist working hard to grow in spiritual awareness, I was trying to prepare myself to receive the Light and Sound of God. Yet all the while I had been littering my consciousness with trash!

*I was trying to prepare myself to receive the Light and Sound of God.*

Wah Z (the inner name of the Mahanta) and the ECK (Divine Spirit) were working with me, both in the dream state and in my waking life, to help me kick the smoking habit. A result of this help was an understanding of the need to drop my cigarettes where they belonged—in the trash.

Now a spiritual ecologist, I dedicate my life to keeping my personal environment clean!

A dream is simply a memory of an experience in the other worlds.

# 8

# Spiritual Freedom

dream is simply a memory of an experience in the other worlds. And often this inner experience is so unlike the day-to-day reality of an individual that it makes no sense to him.

This difference between one's inner and outer reality is a reason some people find it hard to remember their dreams. The irony is that the dream state can also help them. It may reveal a cause that occurred in their lives two or three weeks ago and its effect now, so they can put two and two together. They learn that most personal misery or happiness is of their own making.

An ECKist we'll call Jim had a series of good dreams that told about his spiritual life. The dreams came years apart.

In the first, Jim saw a foundation being laid for a building. But it was of poor construction, and so it all crumbled and was destroyed.

This dream showed Jim's life before ECK. During that stage he had learned the basic rules of how to get along with others, how to esteem life, and how to respect other people's property. That was good. He recognized that overview in his dream. Yet a house not well built may risk collapse. So there had to be a missing element to these basic rules he'd

*A dream is simply a memory of an experience in the other worlds.*

learned about getting along with others, and the like.

But what?

## What Is a Spiritual Dream?

A bit after coming into ECK, Jim had a similar dream. In this one he saw a concrete foundation being laid for a building of incredible size. He realized that this huge foundation meant the teachings of ECK, and he could only imagine what kind of building would rest on top of it.

On the other hand, he sensed it was the temple of his own being.

Sometime later Jim experienced a third such dream. In this one, he saw the same concrete foundation as in the second, but now a framework of steel was rising from it.

This building was indeed his inner temple. Once completed, it would prove to be a mighty temple able to withstand any force.

*Sometimes such a dream makes you ask, "What did it mean?" If it doesn't make sense in a literal way, try to see what spiritual lesson it could hold.*

These are superb examples of spiritual dreams. Sometimes such a dream makes you ask, "What did it mean?" If it doesn't make sense in a literal way, try to see what spiritual lesson it could hold.

Pete, another new member of Eckankar, also tells of a spiritual dream. In it, he was in a room with other ECKists. One said, "Did you drop that letter?" On the floor beside him lay an envelope.

He picked it up. On its front was the address "Holy Child School," the name of a school he had attended as a child. The image "Holy Child School" he took to mean the beautiful state of Soul.

Pete wondered, *What does this envelope mean?*

Then his eyes fell upon another word, *catastrophe,* also inscribed on the envelope.

The dream was pointing to his spiritual exercises. He hadn't done them. And this holy child, Soul, the spiritual being who he is, was missing a golden opportunity to move to higher spiritual ground. He was in fact creating a catastrophe.

The dream shook him.

"But what does it mean?" he asked.

Pete wasn't sure. Although he was aware of skimping on the spiritual exercises, he knew the dream was also about a school he'd once attended, the Holy Child School.

The following night came a dream with hints about the meaning of his first dream. In this one he returned to the school. There he discovered the whole place in ruins, its chalk-white walls weathered by the wear and tear of years. He decided to go upstairs to his old dormitory room, the one place he'd felt most comfortable as a student. Pete tried to climb the stairs, but his legs proved too weak. He couldn't make it up. He crawled, finally, with great effort, and so managed to reach the top.

These two dreams came right before an ECK seminar. During the seminar, it again flashed to mind that he had neglected the Spiritual Exercises of ECK. (These exercises are throughout the ECK writings and are available to all.)

So Pete again began to practice the spiritual exercises.

A half year later, another such dream turned up where he made a return visit to the Holy Child School. This time the school was under renovation. In so many words, his inner bodies—the lower houses of Soul: the Emotional, Mental, and Causal bodies—were being restored one by one.

In the dream he then felt a strong urge to stop

*The dream was pointing to his spiritual exercises. He hadn't done them. And this holy child, Soul, the spiritual being who he is, was missing a golden opportunity to move to higher spiritual ground.*

by the chapel. This place of worship, of course, signified the abode of Soul, Its realm on the Soul Plane.

There he noted the chapel also renewed, its beauty beyond description. Its glory, breathtaking. Very beautiful, snowy white with the Light of God, which at Its highest splendor is of the purest white.

In all its parts, Pete's dream gave an encouraging update to his spiritual progress on the path of ECK.

### DREAM CHARACTERS

Human characters play leading roles in most dreams. They are often people close to you in everyday life and in many cases represent things other than themselves.

Many dreamers gain an insight into personal thoughts or feelings about someone by studying the words and actions of a dream character.

Do you wish to try a technique of dream interpretation?

Upon awakening, then, write down a dream and your thoughts and feelings about it. And pay close attention to the characters you encountered.

*Many dreamers gain an insight into personal thoughts or feelings about someone by studying the words and actions of a dream character.*

## Animal Dreams

Janice, let's call her, kept a kennel for cats as a sideline. People going on vacation brought their feline pets, and she cared for them because she loved cats. She ran a kennel with extra large cages. Her business cards displayed mottoes like "We love cats" or "Love is everything."

She was a real pal to cats.

The kennel thus allowed each cat a lot of space and freedom. Due to the generous individual space, her kennel could host far fewer cats than most other kennels, so business showed less of a profit than it might have. But things done for love do not always show a material gain. Most cats who stayed with Janice relished the visit.

Most all her cats were thus happy. When their owners came for them, they were content to either return home or stay on. Cats know a thing or two about good living.

However, a darkness did once befall this feline paradise.

All the furry guests were happy but for one cat by the name of Busy. To be clear, Busy was a well-behaved cat. For the most part. But whenever Janice left the room, Busy would begin to wail.

Cats can make a terrible racket when they cry, much as some people crying to God (like the Pharisees in the New Testament). An awful howl. Who could stand Busy's laments? Busy sometimes cried on and on. The setup was always the same: whenever Janice quit the room, the cat would loose its dreadful siren.

By the fifth day, her human roommates and her feline guests were going crazy with the noise. The humans ate out just for peace and quiet. But the cats were stuck. Blessed little love remained in this once peaceful refuge. What could Janice do?

She had run this little community as a haven for love. But now, strife.

In the beginning, her kennel was much like God's creation of the world. God put a bunch of Souls on a green or not-so-green patch of earth and said, "You exist because I love you." Then what

*Things done for love do not always show a material gain.*

happened? Centuries of warfare tore loose, with God's darlings on each other with sticks, stones, and words.

What a thankless creation. (Like Busy in our story?)

Soon even Janice lost patience, a surprise because she is a heart person, full of love. But the wailing cat had shattered all peace and harmony.

Janice had scraped the bottom of her patience. So she turned the matter over to the Mahanta. "Mahanta," she said, "I can't do anything. If you or any of the other ECK Masters can help, please do something. The cat's driving me out of my mind."

That night Janice had a dream. In it, she met Prajapati, the ECK Master who takes a special interest in animals. Prajapati went over and began to pet Busy.

As he stroked the cat, a golden heart appeared on Busy's chest, because Busy loved the attention and was soon quiet.

All this happened on the inner planes, in the dream state.

The inner worlds of dreams are as real as this outer physical world. And there's a definite connection between them. Sometimes, if things aren't working right out here, instead of enduring years of karma and trouble, you can get things back on track via a dream. But it takes a certain knowledge to reach the inner worlds.

Here's how: sing the love song to God, HU. In due course, the Mahanta will take you to the other worlds.

The Mahanta may give an experience where you gain an insight either to change your outer conditions or improve your inner self. Sometimes

*As he stroked the cat, a golden heart appeared on Busy's chest, because Busy loved the attention and was soon quiet. All this happened on the inner planes, in the dream state.*

such an adjustment in the invisible worlds is all that's required to make things work better in this physical world.

Soon more ECK Masters appeared in Janice's dream. Busy was happy, running back and forth from one ECK Master to another, enjoying the attention and petting.

Rebazar Tarzs, an ECK Master once from Tibet, picked Busy up and said, "Busy, let's go for a little walk."

Rebazar carried him to a nearby cave.

When they reached the cave's mouth, Rebazar said, "Busy, this is a cave, and we're going inside. It's very important for you to see and understand what this cave means to you."

They walked on in and spotted a cavernous pit. Rebazar explained that Busy had long ago come upon such a pit in a previous life and had stumbled into it. The cat cried in vain for help, but no one heard the cries from the depths of the cave. So the cat perished. The past terror had come into this present life. So it is easy to understand why Busy had a dread of being abandoned.

As Rebazar revealed this past life to the cat, the golden heart on Busy's chest shone more than ever. It now cast a warm glow about them.

"Would you like to explore the cave?" Rebazar asked.

In other words, did Busy have the courage to explore the source of the fear? And, of course, Busy, like most cats, possessed a very inquiring nature. They moved on through the cave. In the meantime, the Light of God poured through Busy's golden heart and lit the pitfalls, holes, and other traps.

Now Janice saw and understood what was

*As Rebazar revealed this past life to the cat, the golden heart on Busy's chest shone more than ever. It now cast a warm glow about them.*

happening to Busy on the inner planes. And never again did the cat have a fit of crying.

Rebazar and the other ECK Masters had brought about a spiritual healing. No small thing to accomplish with a cat. Anyway, Busy's old karma was gone.

*The Inner Master can meet you in your dreams, speak to you, and give all the spiritual direction you need.*

The Inner Master can meet you in your dreams, speak to you, and give all the spiritual direction you need.

### INVITING THE DREAM MASTER

The Dream Master is the Mahanta, the Living ECK Master. He offers help only with a dreamer's permission.

Before sleep, then, give him permission to be with you. Imagine taking your burdens and handing them over to the Dream Master. Then let your mind relax its worries and concerns. Ask him to help clean up the karmic conditions that stand between you and spiritual growth.

Then sleep. Know that you rest in the care of the Dream Master, who will safeguard you and always look to your best interests.

## From Darkness to Light

Truth reveals itself through the Light and Sound of God. Whether it comes to you through an animal, by another person, or straight from the Holy Spirit as Light or Sound, it comes with love.

In a heart full of love, where is there room for fear?

Love dispels fear. When most people enter this physical life through birth, their hearts are open. But after a battery of life experiences, some hearts may pinch shut. Once the heart closes, how will the

Light of God enter? But those who love truth and wisdom will try again to open the heart. They sense something is amiss. They're not whole.

Soul's journey in these material worlds ranges from darkness to light. Soul is Light, a spark of God in this place of darkness. It feels drawn to the source of Its being, which is both Light and Sound.

Let dreams point your way to the truth and wisdom of ECK.

*Let dreams point your way to the truth and wisdom of ECK.*

### Mahanta, I Love You

Do this spiritual exercise before falling asleep, while singing HU or a personal word (for ECK initiates).

Begin with a simple postulate. Let it be an open and easy one like, "Mahanta, I love you."

In the quiet reaches of your mind, continue to sing HU. Let your mind run in a spiritual, automatic mode. This doesn't mean to let the HU song become a mindless repetition of a word. Rather, focus on the Sound Current that resonates within you.

Should you awaken in the night, spiritualize your consciousness again. Place your attention on the Dream Master, the Mahanta, for a second or two.

Then, return to sleep. Easy enough?

Do this exercise with a heart full of love for God. Cherish the divine creation that you are. In this gentle, simple way you become a lover of life.

\* \* \*

*Mike and Bruce's stories are from* Earth to God, Come In Please . . . , *Book 2. See how the magical power of dreams can heal hearts or reveal the future.*

*Names, not the real ones, are added to help you keep track of who's who.*

## HU, a Love Song to God

By Mike DeLuca

My sister Anna in recent times married Will, whose five-year-old son from a prior marriage had died with no forewarning. Ever since, Will had carried a tremendous load of pain from that loss.

One evening Anna, Will, and I were enjoying a discussion about dreams and HU, the name of God in all things. I told how we work with dreams in Eckankar. And further, how we sing the holy word HU to help retain and understand our dreams. Will showed interest. So I went on to say that HU will also heal us of painful ordeals.

"I've often had the beginnings of dreams with my son," he said, "but fear and anxiety shut off the dreams before I can actually meet him."

I suggested he sing HU before sleep.

*Will called in a state of great excitement. He'd sung HU. Then came a dream where he met his son and could pass along many things left unsaid before his son's untimely passing.*

A few days later, Will called in a state of great excitement. He'd sung HU. Then came a dream where he met his son and could pass along many things left unsaid before his son's untimely passing. His son assured him of his happiness.

And that assurance brought Will peace.

Soon after, Will started a local chapter of a national support group for bereaved parents. Because of his comforting experience with HU, he asked me to lead a workshop on dreams and the HU song for this group.

Two at the workshop were a couple from Ireland. Kate and Robert were Roman Catholics

who had moved to the United States a few years
earlier, and whose eldest daughter had fallen ill
here. She died in their arms. The experience
shattered them. They had no support in that
dark hour, because their families were back in
Ireland.

During the dream workshop, Kate and Robert
decided to try singing HU. What was there to
lose? So I led them through a short imaginative
technique in which they were to go to an inner
river of Light and Sound.

When Kate came out of the contemplative
exercise, she said it was the first time in a long
while that she had felt peace.

Back home, they again determined that
nothing could be lost by trying the exercise on
their own. Maybe it could bring an understanding about their daughter's passing. So they sang
HU together and fell asleep. Kate traveled to a
hospital in a dream, where she remained conscious of all that took place. There, she learned
that her daughter was no longer at the hospital,
which Kate understood to mean that the child
was no longer in pain. Later in the dream, she
met her daughter surrounded by a circle of
children.

*In the dream, she met her daughter surrounded by a circle of children.*

"I'm fine," she told her mother. "I don't hurt
anymore. I feel happy, and I have a job to do,
working with these children. It's just wonderful
here."

Kate said, "I just can't wait to bring you to
your dad and tell him all this."

"Mommy," the daughter replied, "I can't go
with you. This is where I belong now. But you
can come visit me anytime you want."

"How?" asked Kate.

"Just do what you did to get here. It will bring you here again," the girl said.

An instant later, Kate was back in bed at home. She reported to Robert all that had happened. The happy couple then told their other children of the dream reunion, and they too began to enjoy dreams with their sister.

A few days after, Kate and Robert attended Bible study class. They reported their healing from the HU exercise. The couple also told Will of their desire to let everyone know the importance of singing HU and asking for help in the dream state.

The HU song and the Mahanta are for all. Singing HU is a great spiritual tool.

Use it anytime.

*The HU song and the Mahanta are for all. Singing HU is a great spiritual tool.*

## How a Dream of Prophecy Came True

By Bruce Weber

The company I work for was going through a rough period. One day it announced a layoff of a quarter of its employees, but six months passed without anyone being fired. Still, anxiety ran high.

I decided not to worry about getting laid off, yet deep down I wasn't sure I'd survive the cutbacks.

One night the Mahanta let me glimpse the direction to take during this uncertainty. In a dream, I stood in the lobby of a skyscraper. I stepped into an elevator. A woman from my workplace was the elevator operator, but in this dream her name was Cassandra. There also seemed to be an unseen person in the elevator with us.

The elevator shot to the top. Then Cassandra opened the doors and announced, "Here is your destination: Hebron."

Hebron? What did she mean by Hebron?

The odd name roused my curiosity as I stumbled off the elevator. I had to watch my footing. The building consisted of only open beams, without walls or flooring, but I saw the sky and felt the wind. A fellow from work leaned against a beam. Odd to say, he wore a safety belt and a chain and was chained to the structure. The next second he'd leaped off and was laughing and flying in the air, borne up by the strong wind filtering through the building.

The tone of the dream was lighthearted. I walked over near my coworker, still aloft in the wind, and said, "Well, that looks like a pretty good idea."

No sooner had I spoken than I noticed a safety belt around my own waist. I picked up the end of a chain on a floor beam, hooked it to my safety belt, and then latched the far end to an iron ring in the wall.

Soon my coworker and I were both laughing and swaying in the wind above the open floor.

I awoke and wondered about the dream's meaning. Doing a little research, I looked up the name *Cassandra* and learned she was a prophetess in Greek literature. She'd resisted the advances of Apollo. So, in retaliation, he doomed her prophecies never to be believed, even though they were accurate.

The name Cassandra in my dream was no doubt a sign for a forthcoming event. My destination was Hebron, which I guessed to be a name of biblical origin—something to do with the Hebrews. A Bible concordance did indeed list such a reference.

*I awoke and wondered about the dream's meaning. Doing a little research, I looked up the name Cassandra and learned she was a prophetess in Greek literature.*

Sarah, the wife of Abraham, had died, and he was about to bury her. With no place of his own to inter her, he approached the people of Hebron. They had great respect for him as a prince of God and so refused his offer to pay for a grave site. They pressed him to take their offer. But Abraham insisted on paying for his wife's resting place. So in the end they relented. And Hebron became the burial place of Sarah and, in time, of Abraham too.

The biblical reference of Hebron was a solid lead.

The message of the dream was that this new floor, or land, was paid for. I had a resting place at my company. Though not bought with money, my employment was secured by means such as service and contacts with fellow workers in my company.

The image of being secured by a safety belt meant to hang tight. If I wanted my job, I could keep it. The winds of change were stirring, but I had the spiritual foundation and job security to enjoy whatever the future held.

Though I had suspected as much in my heart, the dream was of immense help to my self-confidence. Now I could relax, be patient, and soothe my coworkers.

Then came a second realization.

Who was the unseen person with me in the elevator? Who but the Mahanta? He was leading me into a whole new realm of consciousness, to gain a greater perspective of my own future. He stayed close while the strong wind of ECK blew in both my dream and in my career.

True to the dream's prophecy, I kept my position at work. I'm still with the company

*The winds of change were stirring, but I had the spiritual foundation and job security to enjoy whatever the future held.*

after an eventual layoff of 25 percent of the workforce. I have a profound gratitude for that. Thankful for the peace this dream offered during a rough time in my career, I always tell people to ask for the Mahanta's help in their dreams. He can help settle the deepest questions in life. With his guidance, it's possible to catch a glimpse of the answers you need.

The world of dreams is a wonderful place!

Create a dream dictionary. It can help you become familiar with your own dream symbols.

# 9
# Spiritual Exercises for Dreaming

## The Golden Cup

Every evening at bedtime visualize a golden cup by your bed. Its beverage is your dreams. When you first awaken, in a morning contemplation, drink from this cup in your imagination. You are drinking in the night's experiences. It is a conscious way of saying, I wish to recall my night's activities on the inner planes while my body slept.

The golden cup is Soul; it is you. You are one and the same.

As you get in the habit of drinking from this cup, this practice takes on a life of its own. The more the ECK refills this cup, the more Soul (you) shines of Its own golden light. You become an ever-brighter instrument for the Holy Spirit.

Your conscious experiences, day and night, will lead to a greater understanding of your place in the spiritual order of life.

*Every evening at bedtime visualize a golden cup by your bed. Its beverage is your dreams.*

## Your Dream Dictionary

During key times in my life, one of the dream symbols I often saw was a ball field. It was a regular-sized baseball diamond. When everything

149

on the field was in order—four bases evenly spaced, a pitcher, a batter, and two opposing teams—it meant that my life was in balance.

But sometimes the bases lay at odd distances apart and the base path was in less than a perfect square. Or maybe the ball I hit would burst, and a shower of feathers would cover the infield. Again, I might have to chase into the woods to locate first base. Second base might be only a few short steps from first base, while third base could trail off a city block in a random direction.

In other words, everything about the game's setup was wrong.

Upon awakening from such a dream, I could often spot an immediate parallel in my outer life. Something was out of order. The joy and sport had gone from living. There was less happiness.

This sort of dream was a signal to sit down and think up a plan of reorganization. In other words, to discover a way to get back to a real baseball field—with the right distance between bases, the correct number of players on each team, the proper equipment, and so on.

*Create a dream dictionary. It can help you become familiar with your own dream symbols.*

Create a dream dictionary. It can help you become familiar with your own dream symbols. Whether a baseball diamond, a bear, an eagle, a car, the police, a person, or anything else, you'll catch on to a pattern and learn what a given symbol means for you.

Do you want ideas on how to create this dream dictionary?

In a section near the back of your dream journal, or in a separate notebook, keep a list of symbols that appear in your dreams. Add to this dream dictionary of symbols. Log the date next to the meaning you see in each symbol. That allows a way to keep track of changes, as the meaning may shift in time. Allow room for additions.

As you unfold, your dream symbols will spread to new dimensions, a fact unknown to most people who study dreams.

### Two-part Door of Soul

The door of Soul opens inward. No amount of pushing on the wrong side will open it.

Twenty minutes to half an hour is the limit to spend on a spiritual exercise during a session unless an experience has begun. Then, of course, see it through to the end.

To set up an experience with the Light and Sound of God or the Inner Master, use this two-part technique:

1. In contemplation sometime during the day, count backward slowly from ten to one. Then try to see yourself standing beside your human self, which is at rest. Keep this part to half an hour or less.

2. The second part of this technique comes at night when you are preparing for sleep. Speak to the Dream Master, the Mahanta. Say to him, "I give you permission to lead me into the Far Country, to the right places and people."

Now go to sleep. Give no further thought to this technique. Your permission to the Mahanta unlocks the unconscious mind and gives the human mind a chance to retain a memory of your dream travels come morning.

That's all there is to this two-part dream exercise.

Be sure a dream notebook is within easy reach. Keep notes. Remember that in the spiritual field, there is no need to push things. With ECK in your

*The door of Soul opens inward. No amount of pushing on the wrong side will open it.*

life, the gifts of Spirit, like love and wisdom, will now start coming to your attention.

All spiritual good comes with the Spiritual Exercises of ECK.

## Learn about Surrender

In contemplation, say you are an instrument of love for the Sugmad (God), the ECK (Holy Spirit), and the Mahanta. Next, sing HU, the love song to God, for a few minutes.

Listen for a Sound of God, like a buzz or humming pulse, similar to that of an electrical current. These are but two of the many possible sounds of the Holy Spirit. If a Sound comes, then stays with you after the contemplation session, ask the Dream Master, "How can I surrender to this Sound of God?"

*If a Sound comes, then stays with you after the contemplation session, ask the Dream Master, "How can I surrender to this Sound of God?"*

Now imagine a face-to-face meeting with the Dream Master. Listen to his advice about surrender. He will first instruct you to still your thoughts. Then he says to repeat the phrase, "I surrender my whole self to the ECK, the Holy Spirit."

In the morning, jot down any fragments of your dreams. Take them into contemplation right then or at a later, more convenient time.

Did a dream teach anything at all about surrender? If nothing comes to mind, try this exercise again. The messages in your dreams will be easier to read with time and practice.

## To Dream in Full Consciousness

Do you want to learn how to move in full consciousness to a new or higher plane during the dream state? Then try this technique.

Before sleep, place your attention on the Living ECK Master's face. Now try to keep his face in mind as you doze off. Then await his coming as the Dream Master.

In dreamland, anchor your attention on some solid object in the room, like a chair, a clock, etc. Hold that image in mind. Then give yourself a thought command.

Say, *I am awake in this dream.*

Let your attention fix on the solid object chosen as a point of reference above. Feel yourself begin to rise. Layers of clouds like soft cotton puffs will drift past. Thus you shift into a new state of consciousness every bit as real as this physical one.

A shift to a new state of consciousness is a shift to a new plane.

If it's hard to keep your attention on the solid object in your dream, don't worry about it. You will sink into the dream state and later awaken in the usual way.

Another technique to dream in full consciousness is to take the role of a silent witness. Watch others play out their roles, much as you would watch a movie.

Other techniques to try are to start and stop a dream. Or make it more bright or dim. For fun, switch from black and white to color.

Try things.

Still another way to dream in full consciousness is to watch yourself drop off to sleep. Catch the moment of slipping into the dream state.

It does take practice, but it can be restful to your body while doing these exercises of switching into a higher state of consciousness. There need be no trace of fear. You can also rise from one dream level to a higher one, in full consciousness.

A question comes up: What to do if you are in

*Say,* I am awake in this dream.

a conscious dream and want to return to your body? Just feel yourself back in it. That's all there is to it. You will return in an instant.

## How to Get Answers in Your Dreams

At some level, Soul knows all things. If there is something that you'd like to bring down to your day-to-day, waking consciousness, here is a way to go about it.

*Before you go to sleep, relax and decide that upon awakening you will have the answer to whatever question is on your mind.*

Before you go to sleep, relax and decide that upon awakening you will have the answer to whatever question is on your mind. The matter should be of a spiritual nature.

By morning, expect to have the answer in mind.

This is how the process works. At the moment of slipping from the sleep state to the waking, your heart is still open to the night's dream lesson. It is truth, and you are in direct contact with it. At this moment of waking, your answer is within your reach.

Jot down a quick note of the solution in your dream journal. Do it now. Otherwise the answer is lost.

A solution exists for every challenge to our peace of mind. There is always a way, somehow. What holds us back from happiness is our lack of faith in the mighty power of the Holy Spirit to address our most humble needs.

Learn the value of doing a spiritual exercise before bedtime or upon rising. These times work to your advantage while you pursue the expansion of conscious awareness in your dreams.

## Journey on an Ocean of Light

Tonight when you go to bed, shut your eyes and locate the Spiritual Eye. It is at a point right above and between the eyebrows. Now, in a very offhand way, look there for the Light of God, which may appear in dozens of forms.

At first you may see a general glow of light that you think is your imagination. Or the divine light may appear as little blue spots or as a bright spotlight. Or it could look like a beam of light coming in through an open window from the sunshine outdoors.

Any color of light may appear.

As you search for the Light of God, sing your secret word or HU, a name for God which holds great spiritual power.

The word *God* has lost spiritual power by its careless use in profanity and mild oaths.

Watch for the appearance of the Light to turn into an enormous ocean of light much more grand than sunlight reflecting into the eyes from, say, the Pacific Ocean. As this holy Light takes on the appearance of an ocean, keep an eye out for a little boat approaching the shore. At the helm is the Mahanta or one of the ECK Masters. This steersman will invite you aboard. Climb into the boat.

Let any experience follow. Set no limitations. You may, as if by magic, end up in a dream video arcade or inside a Temple of Golden Wisdom. Again, it could be an experience of the Light and Sound of God streaming right into your heart.

Be at peace. You rest in the hands of the Most High.

*As you search for the Light of God, sing your secret word or HU, a name for God which holds great spiritual power.*

# Soul Travel

This Soul Travel experience let him see for himself
that his son lived on in peace and happiness.

# 10
# Soul Travel—Voyages into the Higher Worlds

 aydreams, night dreams, contemplation, Soul Travel—all are steps in the pursuit of heaven.

In Eckankar, an earnest seeker is under the protection of a spiritual guide known as the Mahanta. This is the Spiritual Traveler. As the Mahanta he is the Inner Master, the one who comes on the other planes to impart knowledge, truth, and wisdom. But he also has an outer side. Here he is the Living ECK Master.

Thus, the spiritual leader of Eckankar—the Mahanta, the Living ECK Master—is both an inner and outer teacher for all who wish to learn more of God and life. Such is his role.

So as spiritual guide, the Master helped an African man—via the Ancient Science of Soul Travel—enjoy a reunion with his deceased son.

This man had a teenage son. When the youth was but fifteen years of age, he stepped on a sharp object, got tetanus, and soon died. The father, an ECKist, wished to meet his son on the inner planes. So he went into contemplation and chanted the sacred word *HU* to get spiritual aid. During this

*In Eckankar, an earnest seeker is under the protection of a spiritual guide known as the Mahanta. This is the Spiritual Traveler.*

contemplation, the Mahanta let him move into the Soul body and find his son through Soul Travel.

Father and son thus greeted each other with great joy and love in heaven.

Then the man asked his son a question that had long plagued him, "How did you hurt yourself? What did you step on that gave you tetanus?"

The youth said, "In the corner of the passageway that leads to the kitchen is a nail. That is what I stepped on."

When the father awoke from contemplation, he rose from his bed and examined the passageway. Indeed, in a dark corner near the kitchen, a rusty nail jutted from a floorboard. It was off to the side, but the teen had had the misfortune to step on its deadly tip. The man wrenched the lethal nail from the floor to ensure that no other life would be at risk.

So even while he felt deep anguish from his son's death, this Soul Travel experience let him see for himself that his son lived on in peace and happiness.

*Soul Travel is a gift of heaven.*

Soul Travel is a gift of heaven.

## Like-Minded Souls

Many who embrace the ECK teachings today have in one way or another had some spiritual experiences that their fellows have not. Among them may be near-death experiences, out-of-the-body adventures, Soul Travel, astral projection, or even visions.

In most cases, though, it's better that people not have such experiences day in and day out. Individuals who do are often unable to handle them. In general, they spin out of control, wobbling in their spiritual orbits, causing trouble for themselves and others.

For most people, psychic or spiritual experiences catch them by surprise. They often happen before one has heard of Eckankar. But they do awaken a seeker. With a sense of wonder and self-doubt, he may ask, *What happened? Am I losing my mind?*

So he turns to some authority figure to find an answer to the gnawing questions about his unusual experience. "What happened?" he says. The minister doesn't know. Doctors of philosophy, psychology, or one of the medical arts return blank looks too. Where to now?

Then one day he watches a TV show and learns of others with an extraordinary experience like his own.

"Ah," he says, "all these experiences sound true."

Now our seeker wonders, *Where can I meet people like me?*

Often it's hard to make contact. The TV subjects are from points around the country, and the TV program may not give out names or addresses for reasons of privacy.

But there is a chance to meet others of like experience.

Eckankar is here. Among its benefits is the chance for like-minded people to meet at public seminars. At this open forum, all may learn more of the divine plan behind a variety of inner experiences. The ancient ECK teachings are now available. An advantage of Eckankar and the ECK seminars is that they provide a common meeting ground for all who have had a life-changing experience.

One in three Americans admits to a remarkable experience—either of leaving the physical body or some other phenomenon. Few may have understood its nature, but nonetheless, no one can shake them

*An advantage of Eckankar and the ECK seminars is that they provide a common meeting ground for all who have had a life-changing experience.*

of a belief in its reality. We of Eckankar are here to help them understand. The ECK talks and writings open a window to the mysteries of the higher worlds and what such an experience means.

## What Is Soul Travel?

In the simplest terms, Soul Travel is an individual moving closer to the heart of God. This movement takes a variety of forms.

*In the simplest terms, Soul Travel is an individual moving closer to the heart of God.*

Soul Travel is, for the most part, a tool for use in the worlds below the Soul Plane, first of the true spiritual worlds. It takes one through the Astral, Causal, Mental, and Etheric Planes. As a whole, these are the planes of time and space. Soul Travel occurs in two general ways. One form is the sensation of fast movement of the Soul body through the planes of time and space. In reality, though, is such movement possible?

You see, Soul exists on all planes, so what feels like movement, or travel, is simply Soul coming into an agreement with fixed states and conditions that already exist in some world of time and space.

If you can imagine a scene, then you can be there this same instant in the Soul body. That is the Imaginative technique. It may feel as though you are hurtling through space at a breakneck speed, like a rocket, and zooming on a journey to outer space. In fact, though, Soul (you) is motionless. It is shifting Its attention to some higher state. That shifting of attention results in a feeling of fast motion to the material senses.

Soul Travel begins with a Spiritual Exercise of ECK in a physical setting.

A contemplative may hear a rushing sound, like a wailing wind in a tunnel, along with a sensation of incredible speed. But as explained, Soul doesn't move; Soul *is*. Time and space adjust to Soul's state of consciousness, and it is this adjustment of time and space that renders an illusion of movement or breathtaking speed. A seeming, rapid change of location is one aspect of Soul Travel that may prove to be a daunting obstacle for the timid. These people fear going beyond themselves.

Soul Travel is, therefore, for the bold and courageous in spirit. But remember, since one doesn't in fact travel anywhere, it's impossible to get lost.

Keep that principle in mind during a spiritual exercise. It will lend the confidence to open your heart to love and so delight in any enlightenment that finds you.

Another form of Soul Travel is the expansion of consciousness. This aspect is the true state of personal revelation or enlightenment that we aspire to in ECK. It visits both the timid and the bold, and is a gentler, less robust version of movement in consciousness. Most people experience this sort of gradual shifting of awareness.

Love and wonder define Soul Travel the best.

*Soul doesn't move; Soul is. Time and space adjust to Soul's state of consciousness, and it is this adjustment of time and space that renders an illusion of movement or breathtaking speed.*

## Golden Kiss of God

Soul Travel is thus of several dimensions. Some people describe it as a shift in consciousness. Out of the blue, some event happens to shed light on a spiritual matter that had mystified them. A shift in consciousness to a new plane flits in like a soft, golden kiss of God. Then, these lucky Souls *know* they've had the best of good fortune and have touched the hem of divine love. Rather, it has brushed them.

Soul Travel, as stated, may also be of a more dramatic sort. In this case, an individual transcends the human body and tastes the love and freedom that are a birthright. He rises into the other worlds. Each experience fits him, because each is but a reflection of his spiritual state.

People ask, "Why is it so important in Eckankar to learn Soul Travel?"

Soul Travel, in a broad sense, is of much value because it is a link to the expansion of consciousness. The rule of destiny holds that people at some time will begin to awaken to who and what they are. A knowledge of past lives may also open to them by way of dreams or déjà vu. A few catch a glimpse of future events.

Note that Soul Travel means moving into the higher realms of God, to places people haven't yet dreamed of. Soul Travel reveals a majesty and security that abounds in the arms of God alone.

*Soul Travel reveals a majesty and security that abounds in the arms of God alone.*

For this reason, Soul Travel transcends astral or mind travel, and rote prayer, elevating one into profound spiritual areas. Whenever Soul reaches the far orbits of the inner planes through Soul Travel, the human heart opens to God's all-consuming love.

It is our very purpose to discover that love.

### A Gentle Exercise before Sleep

To travel to your inner worlds, try this spiritual exercise. Do it each evening before sleep. Shut your eyes, then sing HU or your secret word for five or ten minutes. (A secret word comes with the Second Initiation. An individual may request this initiation after two years of study in the ECK discourses.)

Right before dozing off, say to the Mahanta, "Please take me to the place where I can learn all that is good for my unfoldment. Take me to a Temple of Golden Wisdom."

Or say, "Let me see what it's like to Soul Travel; you have permission to help me."

Let a feeling of warmth and goodness fill your heart. The Mahanta is a trusted friend and companion, who loves you as you love him. Be assured of his love, protection, and guidance. You will be safe in every way.

Seekers in ages past discovered and followed a teacher who could guide them beyond the spiritual limitations of body and mind. Countless others, including many saints, have mastered the art and science of Soul Travel. It is in your hands to become adept at it too.

*The Mahanta is a trusted friend and companion, who loves you as you love him.*

\* \* \*

*Julie gets an inside scoop on the Tin Man from* The Wizard of Oz. *Lauretta misses the 1981 ECK Worldwide Seminar, but learn how she meets the new Master. Both stories appeared in* Earth to God, Come In Please . . . , *Books 1 and 2.*

### Finding a Heart of Gold

By Julie Olson

A child of twelve, I had a dream. I was standing in the cemetery near home. One by one, I looked at the children's graves—flat marble slabs the size of shoe-box lids lying level with the ground.

Suddenly I spied an intensely bright gold coin glittering in the dry brown grass. As I stooped to pick it up, I saw other coins scattered in an abundant trail across the lawn. I collected many of them to take home, feeling rich and full of glee. As I picked them up, the trail of gold coins led me out of the cemetery. The dream ended.

The next day, I went to the graveyard after school, half-hoping to glimpse a real gold coin. The dream stayed with me but had no real meaning until almost twenty years later.

\* \* \*

In September of 1986, an unchecked infection raged through my kidneys and bloodstream. My husband and I were living in a new section of our large city, and my physician was out of town. When my temperature reached 106 degrees, my husband took me to a hospital that offered emergency care.

The next four days were a nightmare. The hospital was overcrowded and understaffed. (It later came under federal investigation for incompetent care.) The doctor was unfamiliar with my medical history and couldn't diagnose my problem. I developed a life-threatening case of pneumonia that went completely undetected. I lay in the hospital approaching death, surrounded by medical knowledge and technology.

Each day I thought, *This can't get worse.*

But each day it did. The improper care, ineffectual medicine, and overcrowded room were all part of a carefully crafted divine plan. It wasn't apparent at the time, but I was right where I belonged.

I was never quite conscious. Instead, I felt myself hovering around or above my physical body, not wanting to feel the constant pain and discomfort. Having studied the teachings of Eckankar for fourteen years, I never lost that

*I lay in the hospital approaching death, surrounded by medical knowledge and technology.*

all-important link with the Inner Master. The illness and pain tried to absorb all my attention, but the loving presence of the Mahanta, my spiritual guide, wafted in and out of my consciousness.

It gave me great comfort and security.

However, I began to ask Spirit why I was not getting the right medical attention. What had landed me in this crazy hospital? My husband and parents felt much alarm, since I'd lost the strength to lift my arms. It was hard to breathe. Clearly, I was near death.

Helpless and weak, too ill to demand anything, I couldn't even focus my attention to chant HU, the ancient name for God. Occasionally, just the *H* and *U* would flash together in my inner vision like a neon sign.

On the fourth morning I began to sink. I could feel myself loosening the grip on physical reality and stopped struggling at that point to surrender all.

"Anything is better than this, Mahanta. If I am ready to leave, I will go."

My mind cleared for the first time, and an inner calm descended. It was evident I was close to translating (dying). My body felt like a broken, feverish husk, of no further use. And yet there was a powerful current flowing through me that was not physical. Soul was calm, peaceful, observing, and detached.

As I rose above the pain, I recognized a familiar feeling like floating. I'd felt it many times before during the Spiritual Exercises of ECK and knew I was out of my body—perhaps this time never to return. I kept saying to the Inner Master, "I am ready, I am ready."

*I began to ask Spirit why I was not getting the right medical attention. What had landed me in this crazy hospital?*

There was no emotion, no pull toward family or loved ones, just calm expectancy.

*So this is dying,* I thought.

Then, as if someone had flicked on a movie projector, I saw a scene from the classic movie *The Wizard of Oz.* It registered in absolute clarity upon my vision—every note of the music in perfect pitch and clear, every detail in vivid color far beyond the reaches of Metro-Goldwyn-Mayer.

In the movie, Dorothy finds the Tin Man rusting away in the woods, locked into one position as the years passed. She oils his joints. The sheer joy of movement makes the Tin Man dance. I watched every nuance of the Tin Man's movements, felt every musical note, as pure happiness animated his clunky body.

His joy is unhampered by the awkward shell he wears.

The Tin Man's song is "If I Only Had a Heart." He pleads with Dorothy to take him to the Land of Oz so he can ask the Wizard for a heart, because his creator forgot to give him one.

Every word of the song registered deeply. The scene faded at the end of his song.

As I returned to my physical body, tears rolled down my cheeks. *I* was the Tin Man—encased in a hard shell of physical, emotional, and mental rust. This rust was karma—a shell of pain that had built up through lifetimes of heartbreak and disappointment. Now it was keeping me from my true heart—as Soul.

I asked the Inner Master to help me open my heart to Spirit in this life.

Only the ECK Life Force could soften the karmic rust of centuries. This rust had collected

> *I asked the Inner Master to help me open my heart to Spirit in this life. Only the ECK Life Force could soften the karmic rust of centuries.*

over many incarnations, dating as far back as Atlantis. My heart had been broken so many times as I failed important spiritual tests.

The scene changed, and I was standing in a mist.

Something began to take shape before me, and I became aware of a large, round table. I seated myself at it, alongside several ECK Masters of the Vairagi Order.

Sri Harold Klemp was immediately recognizable, as were Rebazar Tarzs and Fubbi Quantz. A discussion began. I couldn't hear the actual words, but there was a vibration or hum which signaled their conference. I knew the conversation was about me. Presently the discussion stopped, and a question entered my consciousness.

"Julie, what do you want to do?"

A feeling of great love, patience, and compassion surrounded me as their question sank in. Did I want to leave the physical body now? The choice, as Soul, was mine alone.

*Did I want to leave the physical body now? The choice, as Soul, was mine alone.*

Two thoughts cropped up so fast my mind didn't have time to censor them. Soul, the observer, was speaking. One thought was a concern over my husband's anguish and pain. We'd been married only four months. The second thought: I haven't yet met the Soul who just joined our family, which is very important to me. (My sister had just had a baby.)

At that moment my fate was sealed. There was no chance to mentalize the choice; it was made beyond the mind. Soul, the golden heart, had made Its choice. Feeling a sudden surge of purpose and strength, I returned with a rush to my body.

Things moved quickly after that. Within an hour my regular doctor phoned. I was released into his care at another hospital.

The ambulance ride was a lonely one. I felt the weight of my decision as the reality of the physical universe closed in around me. The bouncy ride, the wailing siren, the narrow gurney I was strapped to—all stood in stark contrast to my spiritual visions of the morning. I felt painfully alone.

Ironically, a deep fear of death clutched my heart.

Just then, the ambulance attendant began to sing. Softly at first and then louder, part lullaby and part hymn. I immediately felt the presence of the Mahanta and relaxed. I couldn't see the attendant (and for all he knew I was unconscious), but his soothing voice drowned out the wail of the siren. His unself-conscious song carried the healing force of the divine Sound Current.

*I'm so weak,* I thought, *I couldn't ask him to continue should he stop.* But he kept on singing.

When we arrived at the new hospital, I was caught up in a whirl of activity as my body was hooked up to various machines and tubes. I remained in the intensive care unit for three weeks. It took a full twelve months to regain my health.

The Living ECK Master declared that the Year of Spiritual Healing for the chelas of Eckankar—and many other searching Souls.

\* \* \*

The childhood dream of golden coins returned and stayed with me.

It was a promise made long ago by Spirit. In

*His unself-conscious song carried the healing force of the divine Sound Current.*

this life, Soul would be freed by the Mahanta from the dead traps of ignorance. The karma of many lifetimes would dissolve—lifetimes where I had lost all resonance with myself as Soul. Each golden coin in my dream symbolized a secret gift from the ECK—a key insight into life. These insights would lead me out of the constant round of birth, death, and rebirth, out of the physical plane (the cemetery).

Soul was free of Its earthly bonds.

Eckankar is the path I have chosen to help me gather the golden coins of wisdom in my path. I have the deepest gratitude to the Vairagi Masters and to Sri Harold Klemp, the current Mahanta, the Living ECK Master, for showing me how to use them to open myself as Soul.

I guess you could say the Tin Man found his heart of gold.

### The God Worlds of ECK
By Lauretta McCoy

It was the weekend of the 1981 ECK Worldwide Seminar, and I was disappointed at being unable to attend. But being a creative Soul, I promised myself during a spiritual exercise to visit the seminar in the dream state or through Soul Travel.

That night I had a dream.

I was standing in a place of soft white light when a man drove up in a beautiful, antique, black Model T Ford. It was in mint condition.

*Wow!* I thought, *I really love this car.*

The car in my dream had a certain mystique. It was timeless, better than any modern-day car, and like Soul, nothing could keep it from its journey or destiny. The driver of the car

*I promised myself during a spiritual exercise to visit the seminar in the dream state or through Soul Travel.*

approached me. Greeting each other, we expressed our admiration for the black Model T. He was an average-looking man about my height, dressed in a suit.

"You want to go for a ride?" he asked.

My heart stopped. Just the thought of riding in this car was beyond my wildest dreams. My heart said yes, but doubt crept in. I studied him. *Who is this man? I don't know him.*

"No," I said.

But he didn't seem bothered by my answer and sensed what was in my heart. Taking my hand in his, he said in a kind voice, "Come on and take a ride."

The invitation was extended with much love. I looked at his gentle face, and all doubt faded. I knew it would be all right to go for a ride. Before we climbed into the Model T, he motioned me to follow him to the rear of the car and pointed to a bumper sticker.

It read The God Worlds of ECK.

"Wow! The God Worlds of ECK!" I said and immediately woke up.

*What a wonderful dream,* I thought.

A few days later, my friends returned from the 1981 ECK Worldwide Seminar in great excitement. Eckankar had a new Living ECK Master. One of my million questions was, "What does he look like?" No one seemed able to describe him.

Finally, I drove to the ECK center to see for myself what the new Living ECK Master looked like. There it was, a picture of the kind gentleman who had offered me a ride to the God Worlds of ECK in his beautiful Model T Ford. It was Sri Harold Klemp, the Mahanta, the Living ECK Master.

*Before we climbed into the Model T, he motioned me to follow him to the rear of the car and pointed to a bumper sticker. It read The God Worlds of ECK.*

I knew he was truly the new Living ECK
Master, able to help me grow and explore the
inner worlds of God.

Look around for the Mahanta. He is in the sanctuary—
a dear, old friend of yours.

# 11
# Learning to Soul Travel

nn, let's say, lived in an apartment. She had learned to Soul Travel in her dreams but often wondered why she never traveled beyond her apartment building.

Each time Ann fell asleep and awoke in the Soul body, she could see her physical body lying on the bed. Her routine was to walk through her front door and out into the hallway of the building. There she'd wait. By and by, the Inner Master would appear from around the corner.

"Where do you want to go?" he'd say.

Her usual answer was, "I want to go to a Golden Wisdom Temple." Yet the apartment building was the extent of her Soul Travel journeys.

One night she asked the Inner Master why she never left her living quarters in her dreams. "Please show me what I need to do."

"How did you learn to Soul Travel?" he asked.

So she began thinking about the first time she had found herself out of the body.

## Finding Yourself Out of the Body

During that initial experience with Soul Travel, Ann had walked into the kitchen and the bedroom to look around her apartment.

*"Where do you want to go?" he'd say. Her usual answer was, "I want to go to a Golden Wisdom Temple." Yet the apartment building was the extent of her Soul Travel journeys.*

"Hey, this is great," she'd said.

Each step of the way she'd thought of what to do next. It took her a while in the dream state to think of chanting "Wah Z," the spiritual name of the Inner Master. This name took her to a higher level. Though her intuition urged some new experiment, nothing at first came to mind. But then it occurred to her to sit on the couch and do a spiritual exercise in her dream.

The spiritual exercise took her out of her apartment, into the hallway. There she had met the Inner Master.

That was the first and last experiment she had ever tried.

Finally, Ann understood why the Master didn't come up to her in the dream state and say, "OK, we'll go off to a Wisdom Temple. I'll do everything for you; you don't have to do anything."

The Dream Master wanted her to use her own creativity and initiative.

Most often, someone fails at Soul Travel or dream travel because of a fear of death. Ann started to experiment and have the experience of Soul Travel under her own terms, so this fear began to vanish.

*Soul Travel can be used in every aspect of daily life. It encompasses a lot more than mere travel outside the body.*

In the broadest sense, Soul Travel can be used in every aspect of daily life. It encompasses a lot more than mere travel outside the body. Soul Travel is the expansion of consciousness. It allows one to live each day with more awareness of the greater wisdom and understanding that comes by grace of ECK, the Holy Spirit.

## Answer to a Prayer

Dreams, visions, and other experiences mean little in and of themselves.

Yet in the context of our spiritual life, they are signs of how much we are in accord with life. In fact, the whole point of life is to teach us how to come into agreement with the Voice of God, the Light and Sound. Many find the road to their inner worlds through the teachings of Eckankar.

*The whole point of life is to teach us how to come into agreement with the Voice of God, the Light and Sound.*

Often, however, it takes a personal tragedy to drive us in search of the meaning of life.

Betty (name changed) was a mother, very close to her son; she found Eckankar after his death in a motorcycle mishap. Devastated by the loss, she was unable to find comfort in church. She would cry through the whole service. If she could but feel closer to God, then maybe He would help her understand why the accident had occurred.

More important, where was her son now? Was he OK?

Her prayers for help in understanding were endless.

Five months later, while at her lowest ebb, there came an experience that changed her life. She thought first it was a dream, but it was in fact Soul Travel.

Betty awoke in vivid consciousness in the other worlds. A bespectacled woman with grey streaks in her dark hair met Betty, and they talked for a few minutes.

"Do you know my son?" Betty asked, giving his name.

"Of course I know him," said the other. "He lives right over there in that white house." The scene, a pastoral setting of cottages, looked like a lake resort.

There she found her son, and they had a long conversation. He assured her that his health was better than it had been on earth. Then he looked at her and said, "I know what you're doing to yourself. Please stop. You're hurting yourself."

Before they parted, she asked if she could hold him in her arms, since she didn't get a chance to do so before his death. Merry laughter twinkled in his eyes.

"OK, Mom," he said.

Soul Travel had brought her to him. She could still feel his warmth in her arms when she awoke. Even his scent lingered. A peaceful, happy feeling lasted for weeks before it began to fade. Betty became determined to learn all about her son's new home in heaven. Somewhere on earth, she knew, someone had the answer. That was the juncture where her sister introduced her to Eckankar.

The first book Betty read was *The Spiritual Notebook* by Paul Twitchell. It convinced her that here was the answer to her prayers. Here was an explanation about the other worlds that made sense.

Grief for her son still overtakes Betty on occasion. So she looks to the Mahanta, the Living ECK Master to help her regain the tranquillity she felt while with her son during Soul Travel. She continues to do the Spiritual Exercises of ECK every day.

*Some inner travel techniques are in the ECK dream discourses, which come with membership in Eckankar. More methods are in the book* The Spiritual Exercises of ECK.

Some inner travel techniques are in the ECK dream discourses, which come with membership in Eckankar. More methods are in the book *The Spiritual Exercises of ECK,* available from Eckankar.

Betty now directs her efforts toward seeing the divine Light and hearing the holy Sound—keys to the secret worlds of God.

A story like this may inspire one to look for love and truth. Yet the actual finding depends upon doing the right thing. For those in ECK, it is doing the spiritual exercises, which are in many ECK books and discourses. They take a mere ten to twenty minutes a day. A chant, mantra, is simply a love song to God or a way to key in to the Divine Spirit. A chant helps you appreciate life.

Many ECKists adapt the Spiritual Exercises of ECK to dovetail with their own state of affairs once they catch the knack from the ECK teachings.

### GAZING AT A BRIGHT OBJECT

This technique gets you out of the physical state into a higher consciousness. Just focus on a bright object like a coin, a diamond, a prism, or a crystal.

Gaze steadily at the object. Then imagine going out of your body by feeling light, happy, and full of love.

While thus concentrating, repeat this affirmation: "I am leaving my body. I want to see the Temple of ECK in Chanhassen, Minnesota."

Do this over and over until it becomes so. You will find yourself outside the body, viewing it with joy and amazement. Look around for the Mahanta. He is in the Temple sanctuary—a dear, old friend of yours.

## Key First Meetings with ECK Masters

The mission of Eckankar is to show all the way home to God through Soul Travel and other means.

One's first meeting with the Mahanta, the Living ECK Master may be quite ordinary, an occasion to excite little interest. The moment could slip by without any apparent significance. So the individual

*The mission of Eckankar is to show all the way home to God through Soul Travel and other means.*

misses it, lost among the general conditions of the time and place it occurs.

On the other hand, a first meeting with the Master may have a dramatic impact. Such is the range of effects one may find when approaching the Master for the first time.

A woman from a Sun Belt state of the United States tells of the time she met Wah Z in a San Francisco hotel lobby. It was the mid-1950s. That was some twenty-five years before he took his place as the spiritual head of Eckankar.

A stranger had handed her a copy of *ECKANKAR—The Key to Secret Worlds* by Paul Twitchell. But the book held nothing for her. True, parts of it did support her views on life, but overall she saw little value in it. The stranger had not revealed his identity. And soon, every trace of this incident washed from her conscious mind. It was years later before she recognized him.

Please note, *ECKANKAR—The Key to Secret Worlds* was first published in 1969, about fifteen years after she'd met the stranger in the hotel lobby.

Thirty years after that occasion, in the mid-1980s, she learned his name at an Eckankar meeting. His face was on a book jacket. Only then did she recognize today's Living ECK Master.

*The trials of everyday life temper an individual to prepare for the Master.*

The man looked the same as she remembered him in the San Francisco hotel lobby way back in the 1950s. The memory of that meeting with the Spiritual Traveler rushed in.

It took years of spiritual preparation before her Spiritual Eye opened.

How does her story fit in with Soul Travel? The trials of everyday life temper an individual to prepare for the Master. After this initial, often unheralded, meeting, a seeker begins a long course of training that leads to Soul Travel and the Master.

But little seems to change in everyday things.

## Home to God

Soul Travel is simply the best means for Soul to go home to God. However, some who wish to master it have lesser ideals. They want to learn this ancient science for healing. Others see it as a way to make a fortune, spy on people, steal business secrets, get attention as crime solvers, or earn a living as specialists in lost-and-found items. They harbor every motive except a desire for God.

After an individual first meets the Mahanta, the Master employs the dream state to prepare him for the Light and Sound of God.

Glen, let's say, is an initiate who did a spiritual exercise to reach a certain plane in contemplation. The Inner Master obliged him. The Master lifted him into the far worlds. There, he drove Glen by car through a residential neighborhood at night. The houses rolled by. All at once, the brightest light you could imagine blazed from an empty lot. Its blinding flash was like a magnesium flare.

But the Mahanta knew the pure Light of God could destroy Glen due to his spiritual impurities. So the Master sped by the Light. This quick action prevented injury to Glen's sensitive Spiritual Eye.

At the outset of this experience, Glen had heard the Sound of that plane. It carried him deep into the Far Country. Yet he knew that it takes Light, Sound, and the Master for a full spiritual consummation. The Inner Master had met him. The Sound had lifted him to that high plane. Yet where was the Light? It was necessary to show the way through the dark.

*After an individual first meets the Mahanta, the Master employs the dream state to prepare him for the Light and Sound of God.*

Soul Travel is the line of action that Soul takes on Its final journey home to God. In other words, Soul Travel is Soul's return to Its place of origin. Home.

*Soul Travel is Soul's return to Its place of origin. Home.*

\* \* \*

*Monica learns that love conquers death. Her story first appeared in* Earth to God, Come In Please . . . , *Book 1.*

### Dad's Gift from the Other Side
By Monica Wylie

I was about fifteen when my father died of a heart attack. He'd been born with a heart problem. Growing up, I sometimes felt responsible for my father's painful angina. He wanted to do things with me, but my pace was too fast.

One day while at school, I had a sudden knowingness that my father was about to leave us. I saw him inwardly as he read an Eckankar book.

He said, "I want to rest."

Then in my inner vision, he laid down the book in his lap and translated (passed on) to a higher plane of existence. Sensing my family's concern as it reached out to me at school, I couldn't concentrate in class. Later at home that day, everybody was peering out the window, waiting for me. My mom opened the door.

When I saw her, I knew.

I took my dad's passing badly because I missed him. I missed the hugging and holding, his touch and kindly voice, but because I had grown up with Spirit, the ECK, I wasn't angry. Inside, I knew that his death was simply a translation to a new life for him.

That night, though, I was afraid to go to bed. I'd never been afraid like this before! I wanted to sleep with my mom, but she wanted to be alone. When I got in my bed I felt my father's presence in the room, so I clutched the sheets up to my eyes, ready to cover my head.

Suddenly Dad appeared. He had his white sweater and glasses on, as though he were physically there. As he walked toward my bed, I felt scared—though I sensed he didn't want to scare me.

I felt Dad's gentle voice. "Don't be scared, Monica," he said.

My first reaction was to jump under the covers. As a child, I sometimes saw ghosts in my room, so covering my head with the blankets was an old habit. But after a moment, I pulled the sheet down. Dad was still there. I remember apologizing for being so scared.

*I felt Dad's gentle voice. "Don't be scared, Monica," he said.*

"Don't be scared," he said again. "You know better, now that you've been in ECK for so long."

He came closer. As he walked by my foot, he gave it an affectionate slap. "I love you," he said. His strong fingers hit my foot, just as he'd always done in the morning to wake me up.

Then the vision faded. This visit was Dad's signal that he was off to say good-bye to a few other people.

A friend of my father verified my experience. He'd felt a slap on his back. When he turned around saying, "What the heck was that?" he saw my father. Dad used these familiar touches to let people know he was all right.

I dreamed about Dad too. One night he came to take me dancing.

"No, Dad," I said, "I would rather watch."

As I looked on, he danced with several nondescript beings. I felt his joy at being able to dance, finally free from the pain of angina.

As time went on, we watched each other grow. It wasn't important to my father how I grew up physically, only how I grew spiritually. Dad would drive up in his blue car during a dream or spiritual exercise, and we would visit different heavenly planes. He'd take me to see this scene or that sight in the inner worlds. Sometimes it was to a park.

At our destination, the Inner Master, the Mahanta, would teach us from my father's ECK discourses. We thus progressed through the Astral and Mental Planes.

Now I visit him on the Etheric Plane. He doesn't wear glasses anymore, and he appears thinner and much finer. That's closer to the real him. You see, as he gets higher, I see him more as pure Soul.

One day he said, "I'm not your father anymore; remember that. I only worked as your father on the physical plane. But always remember, the love of being your father is still there. I love you, and you love me, and that's how it is now."

I can't wait to pass this love on to my children.

This Soul keeps teaching me, a gift for which I'm very grateful to the Inner Master. The man who was my father is a Co-worker with God now—that's his true occupation. He's in the inner worlds, though he's also in my heart.

And someday, I'll be a Co-worker with God just like him.

*The man who was my father is a Co-worker with God now—that's his true occupation. He's in the inner worlds, though he's also in my heart.*

He had seen and felt himself in another location, in more than his imagination. No doubt about it. For where imagination is, there is Soul.

# 12
# Beyond Soul Travel: Being, Knowing, and Seeing

*S*oul Travel is simply Soul's movement to God.

This practice is what many devotees of world religions have sought in vain in their own teachings. Soul Travel is an active method of going home to God. The term itself is a dynamic way to express this natural means of ascending to the pinnacle of heaven or plumbing the depths of God's love for Its creation.

Soul Travel is also a cleansing agent for Soul.

Rather than expect you to grasp a full understanding of the philosophy behind Soul Travel, I give stories and examples to tell of its workings. In time, with your own experience as a gauge, you will know what's most important here. The words on these pages are like flower seeds planted in the fertile soil of your heart. You'll remember all you need to, when you need to, for taking a new step toward the infinite love and mercy of God.

Everything has a time and season. So be patient.

*Soul Travel is an active method of going home to God. The term itself is a dynamic way to express this natural means of ascending to the pinnacle of heaven or plumbing the depths of God's love for Its creation.*

Stories are important, because they paint a watercolor for our minds. Like seeds or little time capsules, they burst upon the mind's canvas and add a rich dimension to our recall. So when you need to remember a certain spiritual point, the right story will come to mind. A story can satisfy spiritual hunger in a way that logic cannot.

Soul Travel and the expansion of consciousness make us aware of the effect of our words and actions upon others, and ultimately, upon ourselves.

We make our own heaven and hell.

*Soul Travel and the expansion of consciousness make us aware of the effect of our words and actions upon others, and ultimately, upon our-selves. We make our own heaven and hell.*

## Soul Travel via Imagination

A gentleman once told how as a boy he loved to attend mass. In church, he sat among the other worshipers and marveled at the statues of saints that towered over the congregation on high pedestals. Some statues reached near the ceiling.

*How wonderful it would be to stand beside them,* he thought.

So, while others bent their heads in prayer, this industrious lad did Soul Travel. In the Soul body, he rose above his human body and stationed himself next to the saints, whose heads soared to such heights.

One day, he shared his unique ability with his mother. He confessed how he loved the wonderful experience of rising up near the ceiling by the statues. Why, he could leave his pew and fly up among the saints. Even better, no one could see him. His mother pursed her lips, trying to be clear in her mind on where her son claimed to go.

"You mean in front of the altar?" she asked.

"No," he said. "I mean up there by the ceiling."

"Don't speak such foolishness," she said.

That was that. The boy was still and said no more. Yet he wondered about his mother's reaction to what he had revealed. A frosty ear, indeed.

He had seen and felt himself in another location, in more than his imagination. No doubt about it. For where imagination is, there is Soul. It surprised him to find that others who went to mass never left their pews in their subtle bodies to float around in church. How dull.

*What's the point in going to church?* he wondered.

I tell this story to show that you too can move into the hidden worlds beyond our physical one. It all starts with the imagination. But first, fear and guilt must go. They are like the bricks and mortar of a high stone wall that separates us from our true spiritual rights.

They lock out freedom.

*It all starts with the imagination. But first, fear and guilt must go.*

## Conscious Soul Travel

Our first visits to the inner planes are often in the dream state. On occasion, a few people have the good fortune to begin with Soul Travel, sometimes even before contact with the outer works of ECK.

Earl, let's call him, wrote about a Soul Travel experience of some years ago. It was long before he'd heard of Eckankar or the Spiritual Travelers of ECK.

Earl was then a soldier stationed at a military base. Asleep in the barracks at night, he was often baffled to find himself out of the body, walking through walls. Still, he thought it a fantastic adventure. There were also other times when he left his body. However, his out-of-body travel all took place in the barracks, with no ranging abroad. Yet this ability lent him the unique faculty of seeing through walls and lockers, where he could scan stored clothing and the personal effects of other GIs.

He felt like a man with X-ray vision.

But despite all these early out-of-body experiences, Earl made a curious discovery. He did not Soul Travel after his Second Initiation in ECK. He now describes his state of spiritual consciousness as one in which "I see, I know, I am."

Seeing, knowing, and being.

He speaks of the "I" consciousness which exists on the Soul Plane. Soul Travel is a quick way to move into the higher worlds, but once an individual becomes an inhabitant of the Soul Plane, there is no sense of movement. Perceptions are immediate and direct.

Though all may begin the path of ECK with dreams and then move on to Soul Travel, the day comes when Soul Travel changes to a new method of gaining experience.

Then comes a high state of consciousness—direct perception. It lets us gain experience by the simple mode of seeing, knowing, and being. This change marks one's acceptance as a citizen of the first of the spiritual worlds.

That is the Soul Plane.

*Soul Travel is a quick way to move into the higher worlds, but once an individual becomes an inhabitant of the Soul Plane, there is no sense of movement.*

## The Secret Path to Heaven

The ECK teachings mark the secret path to heaven. The ECK books and discourses brought this spiritual path to light. So do the Spiritual Exercises of ECK and stretch your creative powers. Try a certain technique for a couple of weeks or months to see a spiritual breakthrough. Yes, it may take a while. The human consciousness needs time to adjust so it can receive the enlightenment of God in full measure when it's due. Even without a visual experience of the Blue Light or the Inner Master, you enjoy a divine knowingness. You know that your spiritual life is in good hands.

You just know.

All need not pass through the stage of having to study the introductory ECK works before earning a right to Soul Travel. For some it comes sooner. Past-life training in the spiritual works also comes into play. It affords what appears to be a shortcut to others, who must run the entire course to develop a firm spiritual foundation.

Soul Travel takes you through the psychic worlds. These are the worlds of matter, energy, space, and time. So it stands to reason, within the limits of time, that if you wish to travel, there is distance—space—between here and there. Distance is a separation in time. So it's going to take a certain amount of time to travel from here to there.

In the worlds below the Soul Plane, this concept of time and space is basic science.

However, in the spiritual God Worlds of ECK, from the Soul Plane on up, there is no space as we think of it. Nor is there time. Both are collapsed; they do not exist. So what need is there for Soul Travel?

Soul Travel will carry you only so far, to the Soul Plane, but then you begin to discover the high states of seeing, knowing, and being.

It is there that the real adventure begins.

*Soul Travel will carry you only so far, to the Soul Plane, but then you begin to discover the high states of seeing, knowing, and being. It is there that the real adventure begins.*

## Moving Past Soul Travel

After you learn Soul Travel, a time comes to give it up. It is merely a part of your spiritual evolution.

Those in ECK who show a measure of progress will reach the Soul Plane, a kingdom beyond time and space. It means there is no movement of anything, including Soul. So when you move above the Mental Plane to the Soul Plane, you no longer Soul Travel. It's impossible. There, you develop the skill of seeing, knowing, and being. Instead of movement, therefore, you reach another plane of spiritual consciousness within an instant.

You are simply there.

The Ancient Science of Soul Travel is needed to bridge the gap from the Physical Plane to the Soul Plane.

Some Soul Travel experiences are sensational events. Yet the whole idea of the Inner Master taking you on a Soul Travel journey is to give you a life-sustaining experience needed for spiritual maturity. With it, he proves survival beyond death. Without the Master's help, you will ride the wheel of karma and reincarnation to the end of time.

Thanks to ECK, however, there is a better way. There is the Traveler, the Inner Master.

*Without the Master's help, you will ride the wheel of karma and reincarnation to the end of time. Thanks to ECK, however, there is a better way.*

\* \* \*

*Doug tells of an unexpected visit to loved ones. From* Earth to God, Come In Please . . . , *Book 2.*

### Soul Travel Surprise
By Doug Munson

I sat with my sister, her boyfriend, and about forty other people in an Eckankar workshop on past lives, dreams, and Soul Travel.

Thrilled as I was to be with my sister after an absence of a few years, I still felt an empty spot. I missed my wife, April, and our two boys. They couldn't make the trip to the ECK

Worldwide Seminar with me.

At about two in the afternoon, the facilitators asked our group to try a Soul Travel exercise.

"Place your attention above and between your eyebrows," they said.

This point is the Tisra Til, or the Third Eye. It's a place where Soul—you, as a conscious, individual spark of God—resides.

"Now take a deep breath, and join us in singing HU. It's pronounced like the word *hue*. HU is an ancient name for God; it's sung as a love song to God. Now imagine a place you would like to be right now, just for a moment or two."

I knew where that was—home.

Together our group sang HU. The sound filled the room like a celestial symphony. It spirited me to Minneapolis, to the couch in our living room, where I sat for a second with my hands folded. Then I got up, moved around, and looked in on the boys playing. April was busy with household chores. Although it all seemed to be just my imagination, it still felt real. It felt warm and comfortable to be with them.

But then the facilitators recalled us from the Soul Travel exercise to the workshop. My sister and her friend said they had enjoyed their experiences too.

Then it was off to other meetings.

We three met the next morning to hear Sri Harold Klemp speak. Later, my sister and her friend treated me to a walk along the beach and a quick tour of Hollywood before they drove me to the airport for my afternoon flight home to Minneapolis.

That evening my family greeted me at the

*Together our group sang HU. The sound filled the room like a celestial symphony. It spirited me to Minneapolis, to the couch in our living room.*

airport with hugs and animated stories about the week we'd spent apart. On the ride home I told April all about my sister and that her friend was a nice guy. But I wanted April and the boys to know how much I'd missed them, so I told of the Soul Travel workshop.

"I Soul Traveled home Saturday," I said.

Wide-eyed, she looked at me and said, "What time was that?"

"Oh, a little after two, California time."

"You know," she said, pointing to my younger son, "around four o'clock our time, this little guy said, 'Mommy, I just saw Dad in the kitchen with you out of the corner of my eye. He was standing next to you with his hand on your shoulder.'"

Allowing for the difference in time zones, it was the exact same time.

*"I Soul Traveled home Saturday," I said. Wide-eyed, she looked at me and said, "What time was that?"*

Soul Travel incorporates many experiences from the inner worlds and weaves them into a tapestry of exquisite beauty and value beyond price.

# 13
# The Light and Sound
# of God

n old misunderstanding about Soul Travel is that it is nothing more than a simple occult projection out of the body, into the Astral Plane. Yet Soul Travel is an all-inclusive skill. It goes well beyond the Astral Plane and into the Causal, Mental, and Etheric Planes. Then, right on to the Soul Plane.

Soul Travel is thus a modern way to speak of Soul on Its journey home to God.

Several phases one may expect in ECK include dreams, visions, Soul Travel, the ECKshar consciousness, and God Consciousness. Each of these facets reflects a magnification of God's Light and Sound for the traveler.

Each phase of spiritual attainment in ECK offers a set of experiences, and each phase leads to a higher plane.

A vision, to cite an example, is a pre–Soul Travel event. An individual, still bound to the physical body, hangs back from admitting to an all-out search for God. All the more so if it means leaving the security of the human shell. So the light of truth slips in upon him with a vision. A vision is a promising start

*Soul Travel is an all-inclusive skill. It goes well beyond the Astral Plane and into the Causal, Mental, and Etheric Planes. Then, right on to the Soul Plane.*

toward the Kingdom of God.

Our goal is God-Realization in this lifetime.

*Our goal
is God-
Realization in
this lifetime.*

## There's More

An example of a vision is this report from a doctor in California.

In contemplation, he relaxed and declared he was a channel for the Mahanta, the Sugmad (God), and Sat Nam (mighty ruler of the Fifth, or Soul, Plane). He was ready to quit his contemplative session after a bit, as no results were in sight. Then, in his Spiritual Eye, a flood of colored rays beamed from heaven and into him. The different colors, he judged, stood for the Mahanta, the Sugmad, and Sat Nam.

Then a voice said, "That's not all there is."

A strong impression told him that a missing part of his declaration at the start of contemplation was the all-important ECK, the Holy Spirit of God. So he now declared himself also a vehicle for the ECK, and thereupon the heavens filled with the Light and Sound of God.

"A wonderful experience," he said.

If one has a vision of this kind, he is beginning to see the deeper secrets beyond the reach of the human eye.

### A REMINDER

If you wish to Soul Travel at night while your body sleeps, remind yourself of this desire a few times during the day. For example, tell yourself, *Tonight I will Soul Travel in my dream.*

Your mind will better accept an idea if it's repeated throughout the day.

Now visualize the sort of dream you would like. Make believe it's real. Picture the dream, picture its results. You may also play a movie scene in your mind of the advice or help you seek from the Dream Master.

## Dreams Lead to Soul Travel

The dream is a natural, early phase of training that the Mahanta, the Living ECK Master employs to instruct a student.

Soon the individual finds the makeup of his dreams changing from pre-ECK days. The fogginess, the pointlessness, of dreams begins to clear. The sunlight of truth now beams in. So one senses a new direction in his inner worlds; it brings into being dreams of clarity and meaning. The dream state is thus a basic part of the Mahanta's teaching. To be sure, there are no clear-cut boundaries to mark out the multiple levels of experience.

So an ECKist, one far along in initiations, may report what on the face of it appear to be ordinary dreams or run-of-the-mill visions.

As a rule, though, this is seldom the case. He's moved on. The closer an initiate of ECK comes to God, the more he lives and moves in full consciousness. A unique state of awareness is his signature in every world he enters.

Dreams and visions are a fascinating subject. Yet an ECKist finds that Soul Travel probes a lot deeper into the riddle of life than do any astral or mental projections.

Hence his goal is total awareness, and he puts away the toys of psychic phenomena.

## Visiting Inner Worlds

The next example shows a two-part play of ECK: giving and receiving. It starts with a dream and moves on to Soul Travel.

*The dream is a natural, early phase of training that the Mahanta, the Living ECK Master employs to instruct a student.*

In a dream, then, the Mahanta handed an ECK dreamer a photograph of the dreamer with two young men. All stood next to a lamppost. The dreamer handed them something. When he awoke, the meaning of the dream was clear: He was giving light to these two individuals, as shown by the lamppost.

The dream's images left no doubt.

Yet this dream led to a second occurrence. To better understand his dream, this ECKist went into contemplation but soon fell asleep.

He awoke in Sat Lok, the Soul Plane. This was more than a commonplace dream. This experience was an actual visit to the dividing line between the material worlds and the spiritual planes. Rebazar Tarzs met him there. This wonderful ECK Master had taken a special interest in him, showing him the way to spiritual maturity. Rebazar told this devotee that he'd now gained enough understanding to teach ECK to others.

*The message was for the dreamer to get into the mainstream of life.*

The message was for the dreamer to get into the mainstream of life.

The dream experience by the lamppost had led to a visit to the Soul Plane. Notice, there is no sharp line of demarcation between the dream phase and the Soul Travel experience that followed. For Soul Travel was indeed the second part of this event.

All in all, visions and dreams lead the way to Soul Travel, though it's no fixed rule.

This crossing from dreams to Soul Travel is a major development in our spiritual lives. It marks a conscious effort to travel into the far worlds of God, a desire in line with the aim of Soul.

Our mission is to become a Co-worker with Sugmad, the God of all. Thereby we gain an ever-greater love for and awareness of the Creator, Its creation, and every creature within it.

Soul Travel is thus the most direct way to see the heavenly worlds inside us.

## Light and Sound

Yes, for the most part, Soul Travel is a function of the lower worlds of matter, energy, space, and time. Yet it is the most direct way to pass through the material worlds to the spiritual realms above. So it is a valuable tool.

Almost anyone can learn it. All it takes is an earnest desire and the drive to realize the Kingdom of God here and now, in this very lifetime.

Soul Travel is therefore a bridge. It arches over the gulf that keeps the human from the divine. It is a natural but unrecognized talent that develops with the Spiritual Exercises of ECK.

Here follows an example of how Soul Travel may lead to a higher spiritual state.

A chela in Africa lay down in bed, covered his ears with pillows, then listened for the Sound of ECK. Listening for this holy Sound is very much a spiritual exercise. Like a sweet, though rushing wind off in the distance, this divine melody seemed at once both near and far. In fact, it was inside him. Soon came the sensation of a gentle tugging at the top of his head. He stayed calm. Then came a total liberation from his human shell.

In the magnificent Soul body, surrounded by love and goodwill, he hovered over his human form in bed with wonder.

"The whole of this space was lighted with shimmering atoms and bright giant and small stars," he said.

*Soul Travel is thus the most direct way to see the heavenly worlds inside us.*

He studied his appearance. To his great joy, he found the radiant Soul body alive with energy and power.

Now he sang "Sugmad" in a gentle lullaby. Thereupon he knew that all the glittering atoms and stars were a part of him. As he sang, energy began to vibrate from inside him, flowing out to sustain all things and beings in this unending universe of stars. What tremendous love and mercy he felt for all beings in this expanse of light!

A great Sound now arose from his breast. It touched and granted bliss, life, and power to all in his worlds. That, in turn, lifted him into a spiritual ecstasy, due to his act of giving love and mercy to all.

Now and again the ecstasy returns.

The experience was one of brief homage to the Sugmad (God). It still enriches his life in every way. This experience began as Soul Travel. Indeed, it went far beyond, turning into a spiritual journey to the high worlds of God. And yet, the hem of God's garment is not the whole of it.

*If the full God experience came to one without preparation, it would cause a setback of long duration.*

If the full God experience came to one without preparation, it would cause a setback of long duration.

## Leaving the Body

A classic Soul Travel experience sees one leave the human body in full awareness, with the Light and Sound of God streaming into the Soul body.

Some people have done that in an earlier life and need not learn the ABCs of Soul Travel. But the Mahanta gives them a brushup course. It acts like a springboard to the holy states of seeing, knowing, and being. To see, know, and be are qualities of Soul at the foreground of our attention on the Soul Plane and higher.

These three attributes are the fruit of the ECKshar consciousness.

Soul Travel thus starts with one's state of consciousness today. It takes the human consciousness and stretches it, giving a person a new, deeper insight into the wonder and complexity of creation.

Now let's look at a striking, but rare sort of Soul Travel. It shows how this ancient science blends into the affairs and circumstances of each seeker's makeup.

Michael from Ghana once had an experience that shook his beliefs about physical reality. The experience raised some questions. Those concerns led him, in the several years to come, on a search for answers.

Michael has a practical mind, albeit a very complex one. So an ECK Master sent him on a unique out-of-body trip to challenge and expand his understanding.

Michael had heard and read about people in Ghana, non-ECKists, who'd become lost in strange, invisible, and mysterious towns that they claimed did not exist. Their experiences confounded them. After they told their tales, it was next to impossible to believe them. Moreover, there were also stories of people who'd died but were reported in encounters in other parts of Ghana. Sometimes these "dead" people vanished into thin air when a living person confronted them.

But none of that was on Michael's mind on that ordinary day as he set out on some personal errands in the city of Accra.

A taxi dropped him off at his first stop without incident. His business in the government office lasted

*Soul Travel takes the human consciousness and stretches it, giving a person a new, deeper insight into the wonder and complexity of creation.*

ten minutes. The next stop was a short distance away, along a tree-shaded street, so Michael decided to walk. From there, errands done, he took a fancy to walk home.

That is where he entered a twilight zone.

A tall, stout man of thirty-five called to him from behind. "Do you know the location of the Ministry of Education Annex?"

Michael said no. They parted ways.

Five minutes later Michael was lost. He thought he knew the streets of Accra like his hand, but the unfamiliar streets and buildings around him were a labyrinth of confusion. What was going on? Michael asked directions. He followed one through a narrow lane set between a house and a mansion.

His position was hopeless. What part of Accra could this be?

The experience ran on, taking him outside the city to a suburb. But that town lay in the wrong direction. Petrol (service) stations, churches, the city's traffic circle—all familiar locations—were either gone or changed in appearance.

Poor Michael. To say he was in a confused state is to make light of his misfortune.

Nor could he retrace his steps. Streets were new or laid out in a different way. Worse, the service station of a few minutes ago had vanished, as had a beer bar with a blue canopy over the door. Michael only broke free of this experience after he caught a regular city bus from that suburb to Accra.

Later, he could not duplicate the route of his strange journey into an even stranger dimension.

Of course, it perplexed him.

He'd never read of anything like it in the ECK teachings, but he drew a few conclusions on his

*Errands done, he took a fancy to walk home. That is where he entered a twilight zone.*

own. First, was it possible that this physical plane had many levels that are kept separate from each other by different vibrations? Can such exist side by side, invisible to each other?

Yes, it's true. No absolute line of demarcation separates the Physical Plane from the Astral Plane, so the very top vibrations of the physical world blend into the lower astral region beyond.

Then crossover visits occur.

Second, the question, When did he enter the invisible world?

He concluded that it all began when the tall, stout stranger called to him from behind. (That stranger was an ECK Master. He'd come to help Michael expand his state of consciousness in a manner that fit Michael's state of awareness.)

To sum up, this otherworldly experience began with the stranger and ended with Michael on a bus back to familiar grounds in Accra.

Of interest here is that Michael could not escape this strange morass of events without the impartial aid of a bus driver. To be sure, this was an uncommon Soul Travel experience. Yet it taught Michael that the stories he'd heard about strange towns and people in Ghana were true. A Westerner might have a good laugh at such a tale, but the people of Ghana know better.

And so does Michael.

Beginners in Soul Travel like to stay close to the body. It gives them confidence. So the Mahanta or another ECK Master will help them shed the human state of consciousness and stick to a short journey into a higher plane.

An experience like this may include a feeling of moving out of the body, of floating through a ceiling

*No absolute line of demarcation separates the Physical Plane from the Astral Plane, so the very top vibrations of the physical world blend into the lower astral region beyond.*

or wall, or even of flying into space.

A glimmer of light shines at the remote edge of this space. The Spiritual Traveler guides the novice toward it, and they emerge into a most novel setting. There an intriguing world beguiles the newcomer.

The new Soul Traveler may there explore city streets that are much like those on earth. The people, however, go about duties unknown to earth.

For example, some of them greet arrivals who have died on the Physical Plane to resume spiritual lessons on the Astral. Others guide Souls who visit the Astral Plane during dreams. Whatever duties the Astral Plane dwellers perform, they all serve the spiritual hierarchy in many vital ways that make life go around, as do people in every part of God's vast kingdom.

## Riding the Wave Home

*This deep insight into the workings of everyday life is more important than any single experience out of the body.*

Soul Travel is a very enriching part of Eckankar. Its main benefit is to let us tap into the wisdom and knowledge we've gained in the other worlds. Thus we may enjoy a heightened state of awareness twenty-four hours a day.

It is in this way that the inner and outer experiences build upon each other, to bring more love, joy, and understanding into our lives. This deep insight into the workings of everyday life is more important than any single experience out of the body.

However, Soul Travel incorporates many experiences from the inner worlds and weaves them into a tapestry of exquisite beauty and value beyond price.

That is Soul Travel.

In Eckankar, we turn aside from false authority.

We acknowledge only the real guidance that rises from the heart. The power to do so comes from the Mahanta, the Living ECK Master. If you meet with a Soul Travel or out-of-the-body experience, don't ask someone else to validate it. You are the sole judge. Prove your own experience. You alone must determine its value.

Beyond its exciting side, Soul Travel is a direct way to hear the Sound and see the Light of God. That cannot be done from the human consciousness. The Sound and Light are the wave of divine love that Soul catches into the kingdom of heaven; they are the twin aspects of the ECK, the Holy Spirit.

The ECK is the Voice of God, the Comforter, the spirit of truth.

*By the time one learns the secrets of visions, dreams, Soul Travel, and the ECKshar consciousness, he is an experienced traveler in the high regions of God.*

By the time one learns the secrets of visions, dreams, Soul Travel, and the ECKshar consciousness, he is an experienced traveler in the high regions of God.

Then comes the crown of realization, the enlightenment of God.

Experience is our hallmark in ECK. An individual may read all the books on faith and spirituality in a metropolitan library, but reading nets him nothing in the God Worlds. Only experience goes beyond the detours and dead ends of life. Only experience reveals the correct road to the realm of the All.

So a milestone in Soul's supreme journey to God is the art and science of Soul Travel.

### A Gateway to Soul Travel

If you want to learn Soul Travel, do this technique tonight. Before sleep, shut your eyes and place your attention on the Spiritual Eye. It's right above and between the eyebrows.

Then sing HU. Fill your heart, mind, and body with warm love.

This feeling of love grants the confidence to venture into some new, unexplored area of your spiritual being. A way to fill yourself with love is to call up a warm, comfy memory, like a child's hug or a mate's kiss.

Just so the feeling warms your heart with deep love.

Now, eyes still shut, look into the Spiritual Eye for the holy person who is your ideal, whether Christ or an ECK Master. In a gentle voice say, "I give you permission to take me to the best place for my spiritual good."

Then chant HU, God, or some other holy word.

Next, see yourself in a familiar place, like a special room in your home. Be assured that the guide who comes is a dear, long-standing friend.

Do this session five or six times over as many days.

*A spiritual exercise is like a physical exercise in that all muscles need time to respond.*

A spiritual exercise is like a physical exercise in that all muscles need time to respond. So, do this spiritual exercise at least a week before throwing in the towel. Success comes with diligence. And if you do an exercise routine for a couple of weeks, you may surprise yourself at your new spiritual outlook.

Thus, the same kind of discipline applies to both physical and spiritual exercises.

The sole purpose of the Spiritual Exercises of ECK is to open a conduit, or channel, between you and the Holy Spirit, the Audible Life Stream. The origin of this wave is the heart of God. The moment you begin to sing HU and look for truth in this particular way, changes of a positive nature do awaken within you.

You may not see them at first, but your friends and family will.

\* \* \*

*Death has a long arm, as Rhonda saw, but the reach of life is longer still. This story is from* Earth to God, Come In Please . . . , *Book 2.*

### A Death That Changed My Life
By Rhonda Mattern

In 1986, I married a French ECKist. I remember thinking how bizarre, yet wonderful it was to spend my entire wedding reception seated in a corner with my new mother-in-law. We discussed Eckankar in French.

My mother-in-law, whom I'll call Sophie, felt alarm over her son's involvement in Eckankar. During our conversation, she interrogated me about each wedding guest.

"That man over there in the nice suit. Is he in Eckankar?"

"Oui, Sophie."

"And the woman from Togo; I hear she's a lawyer. Is she involved in this too?"

"Oui, Sophie."

"And the doctor from Versailles? He's in ECK?"

"Oui, Sophie."

She was incredulous. How could all these normal people be involved in something she thought so strange?

*The moment you begin to sing HU and look for truth in this particular way, changes of a positive nature do awaken within you.*

Over the years, Sophie and I had many heart-to-heart talks about ECK and other subjects. She even read an ECK book or two, and though she became more comfortable with Eckankar, she remained a skeptic.

My husband and I divorced in 1992 but remained good friends. I stayed in touch with his parents, planning to visit them after the 1992 ECK European Seminar.

A few weeks before my trip to Europe, I got an urgent call from my ex-husband. My heart raced as I tried to make sense of his news: His mother, Sophie, had committed suicide. My mind rushed in five hundred directions at once. Sophie, vibrant and beautiful. Sophie, the woman with everything—the right car, the right husband, the right house on the French Riviera, the right clothes.

I hung up the phone in a daze. For hours I paced from one end of my apartment to the other, crying uncontrollably. Somehow it was hard to accept the fact I would never see her again.

"Wait a minute!" I said. "I *can* see her again!"

Conscious Soul Travel had never been my strong point. Although my years in Eckankar brought many incredible out-of-body experiences and lucid dreams, I can rarely bring them on at will. However, in this moment of despair, I felt a new determination to brave the inner planes and see Sophie one last time.

I lay down on my bed and sang HU for a few minutes. Try as I might, nothing happened. I felt ashamed that after eighteen years in Eckankar, I still hadn't mastered the art of Soul Travel.

Once again, waves of sadness and loss washed over me, emotions that my mind labeled as nega-

*Somehow it was hard to accept the fact I would never see her again. "Wait a minute!" I said. "I can see her again!"*

tive. As I tried to push back these negative feelings, my mind drifted to a passage in one of Paul Twitchell's early books on Eckankar. In it, Paul finally succeeds in initiating a meeting with his teacher, the ECK Master Rebazar Tarzs. The secret, Paul found, was to travel on a vibrational field on the inner planes between himself and his teacher.

With a start I realized that the key was not putting aside my feelings, but using them as a way to travel to Sophie.

My feelings were beautiful, deep, and totally fitting for the moment. They were a wave issuing from my heart, a wave to ride into the higher worlds.

With this in mind, I began to focus on my love for Sophie. I felt myself lifted in a dizzying, spiraling motion. Before long I stood on a cloud, with a confused-looking Sophie beside me.

*A cloud*, I thought.

*How corny. This can't be real. Where are the temples, the Masters? This is just imagination.*

Sophie was astonished to see me. She spoke to me in excited French.

"Rhonda, it's you! Am I still alive?"

"No. Well, *yes*. I mean, you died, but as Soul you're still alive."

"Why are you here? Are you dead too?"

"No, I wanted to visit you."

"So this Eckankar, it's all true, then?"

"Oui, Sophie."

In the conversation that followed, Sophie and I discussed the guilt she felt on committing suicide. The whole time I was talking to Sophie, part of me stood back, taking a critical look at this experience.

*I began to focus on my love for Sophie. I felt myself lifted in a dizzying, spiraling motion. Before long I stood on a cloud, with a confused-looking Sophie beside me.*

*This can't be happening,* I thought. *I must be making it up. I don't really have the ability to consciously Soul Travel.*

Suddenly, Wah Z (the spiritual name of Sri Harold Klemp) was by our side, glowing in a blaze of white light. I told Sophie I would like to introduce her to someone very special. She saw Wah Z and said, "Oh, it's the head of Eckankar. C'est la grosse légume [the big vegetable]."

This struck me as a funny comment, but so much was happening that I simply brushed it aside.

The three of us stood in a circle and hugged. I could hear sounds swirling around us and felt a love that words cannot tell. I wanted to stay in that moment forever, but try as I might, I couldn't hold on to the experience.

Suddenly I was back in my bedroom.

Rooted once more in the physical world, I started to doubt my experience. Each time a doubt would crop up, I'd hear the words *la grosse légume.* After a number of rounds of this, it occurred to me that a message from Divine Spirit was trying to get through.

I called a French friend. "Is *la grosse légume* a standard expression in French?" I asked.

He explained that "the big vegetable" was the equivalent of "the big cheese" in English. That made sense: Sophie loved to joke and tease. I could picture her seeing the Mahanta for the first time and referring to him as "the big cheese of Eckankar."

Suddenly I froze. Wait a minute. I didn't know that expression in French. But Sophie did. That meant she *was* there.

*The three of us stood in a circle and hugged. I could hear sounds swirling around us and felt a love that words cannot tell.*

My experience must have been real!

As the weeks and months pass, my mind still questions: Maybe I heard *la grosse légume* in conversation once and filed it away unconsciously. Maybe it was in a book. Maybe I knew it once but forgot it.

But as Soul, I know the truth. Last month, once again, I rode the waves of love to visit a dear friend on the inner planes.

*As Soul, I know the truth.*

One day you'll find yourself in a higher state of consciousness, exactly as you acted it out so many times in your imagination.

# 14
# Spiritual Exercises for Soul Travel

hether Soul Travel fits one's spiritual needs is his business. If his heart says yes and he wants help, that's mine. I'm here to help.

## Our Inborn Desire for God

Soul Travel puts zest into life. It is the most direct way to ease the spirit of yearning for God planted in every heart at birth.

"Seek God," says the heart.

Each awakening Soul is like the seeker in *Stranger by the River*. Listen to author Paul Twitchell:

"Outwardly, [the seeker's] life was little different from that of other people—working, toiling, laboring—yet his struggle to find life was deeper and more acute; the pain was greater, the suffering unbearable, and his sensitivity more intense.

"Nothing could lift him spiritually, and the responsibility or success which other men had would not touch him. He was the outcast, the lonely, and the dejected, for love had passed him by as there was nothing in his life which love had to anchor upon."

*Soul Travel puts zest into life. It is the most direct way to ease the spirit of yearning for God planted in every heart at birth.*

215

Then a beam of grace lit the seeker. He met the Spiritual Traveler. And with the Master came divine love.

If the seeker's quest should ring a bell in you, try the following exercise, "The Easy Way."

### THE EASY WAY

Just before sleep, place attention upon your Spiritual Eye. It is between the eyebrows. Then sing HU or God silently.

Fix attention on a blank movie screen in your inner vision, and keep it free of any pictures. If unwanted mental thoughts, images, or pictures do flash up on the screen of your imagination, replace them with the face of the Living ECK Master.

After a few minutes of silence, you may hear a faint clicking sound in one ear, perhaps like the sound of a cork popping from a bottle. You will find yourself in the Soul form in a most natural way, looking back at your physical body in bed.

Now, would you like to go on a short outing?

There is nothing to fear, for no harm can come to you while outside the body. The Mahanta will be with you to keep watch over your progress and offer support. After a while, the Soul body will return and slide gently into the physical self.

That is all there is to it.

If this exercise is not successful the first time, try it again later. The technique works. It has worked for many others.

*If this exercise is not successful the first time, try it again later. The technique works.*

## What Is Soul Travel?

"Soul Travel is an individual experience, a realization of survival," says *The Shariyat-Ki-Sugmad,* Book One. "It is an inner experience through which comes beauty and love of all life. It cannot be experienced in rituals and ceremonies, nor bottled in creeds."

Realization means to be fully aware of something.

Proof of Soul's survival comes every time a person goes to sleep. Sleep is an out-of-body experience. Few realize that. Proof of Soul's survival is in the awakening, and thus sleep may be called "the little death." During sleep, Soul leaves the physical body and travels to some other place. It then returns, and the body awakens.

*Proof of Soul's survival comes every time a person goes to sleep. Sleep is an out-of-body experience. Few realize that.*

Yet to the average person, this natural process of Soul's comings and goings is an unconscious act. The enlightened ones, however, are in full control of the process.

Realization, like experience, is an individual matter.

Much misunderstanding and fear exist about a God-given ability like Soul Travel. To protect itself from the insecurity of the unknown, the public girds itself in fear. It weaves a web of hostility to contain the unknown and so tries to isolate itself with a net of superstitions.

The average man on the street treats the unknown with more than a trace of suspicion.

Realization, at its core, is the other side of ignorance. Realization parts the curtain that separates truth from lie, fact from fiction, and the known from the unknown. The curtain is of the Kal's manufacture. The Kal Niranjan is the king of negativity, and his job is to keep all Souls in ignorance. He hides from them their everlasting nature.

Soul, the ever awakened, exists beyond the sleep state of the human consciousness.

*To take a new viewpoint about something brings understanding about the little things of life. Soul Travel means moving into a new, higher state of consciousness.*

To take a new viewpoint about something brings understanding about the little things of life. For example, a woman wrote to say that Soul Travel was in one instance a very subtle experience for her. Yet the outcome produced a major shift in consciousness for her.

Note the practicality of Soul Travel in the following story.

She tells of her parents well along in years. Both are in their nineties. For fifteen years, she went to their home once a week for lunch or dinner—to keep an eye on them and stay in touch. It occurred to her how much she'd learned from them over the years.

One week, the three had a talk about elders and the day they're unable to care for themselves. Wouldn't their children, with the best of intentions, invite them to come live with them or move closer?

Her parents gave their view of this seemingly generous offer.

They would not want to move. If they did, everything would be new, and they wouldn't know anyone. They'd have to start over. A move meant a new church, new doctors, new friends—a high-stress change for younger couples in good health. But they, with far less energy than the young, would meet too much stress for comfort.

The daughter, of course, got the point. She could see how her well-meaning intentions would look from her parents' side of the curtain. So she left well enough alone. She respected their wishes to stay in their present home.

A clear realization, it was nonetheless a far-from-dramatic kind of Soul Travel.

Soul Travel means moving into a new, higher

state of consciousness. Its result is always of positive effect. By sprinkling light on darkness, Soul Travel brings love, wisdom, and freedom to all it touches.

Soul Travel, therefore, is a means of changing an old viewpoint to a new, higher one.

If you want a down-to-earth exercise of Soul Travel, you'll like the next one, "Around the Room." Stick with it. Then watch your state of awareness stretch and grow into one of a greater love and appreciation, for you'll find the spiritual treasures already within your grasp.

It'll be your little secret.

*If you want a down-to-earth exercise of Soul Travel, you'll like the next one, "Around the Room."*

### AROUND THE ROOM

This spiritual exercise uses the imaginative body.

Take a seat in a chair in your kitchen. Make yourself comfortable. Then say, "I shall go for a short walk in the Soul body."

Shut your eyes. Look into the Spiritual Eye in a soft, sweet, gentle way. Sing HU for a minute or two. Now, in your imagination, see and feel yourself stand up from the chair.

If I were to do this contemplation, I would say, "I shall rise from the chair in my Soul body and walk around the kitchen table."

Then I'd study the kitchen, the color and pattern of the tablecloth, and the flowers in a vase. Also, the fruit bowl on the counter, and the bread box.

While the physical body continues in contemplation with eyes shut, I'd walk to the window in the imaginative body and feel the texture of the curtains. Feel the softness of the yellow cloth.

So be curious. Decide to see what's below

the curtains. Observe the place where the curtains meet the windowsill. Pay close attention to small details of objects around the kitchen.

Now walk to the door. Touch the doorknob. Notice what it looks like in design and color. Before turning it, however, say, "On the other side of the door the Inner Master is waiting." Open the door. Sure enough, he's there. He looks like his photo. His eyes, too, show the familiar love and warmth.

"Are you ready?" he asks. "Let's take a walk outside."

You and Wah Z (my spiritual name) take a walk and admire the sights along the way. Strike up a conversation with Wah Z. Forget the heavy spiritual topics for now. Point out the beauty of a flower, for example, or the melodic song of a bird.

When you want to return to your physical body at rest in the kitchen chair, tell him so.

"Wah Z, may we go back to the kitchen? I want to see myself in the chair." Then go inside to the kitchen. All through this experience, sing HU or your secret word.

When you enter the kitchen, look at your human body, then say, "See you later, Wah Z. I'm going to sit down in the chair and get myself together." (A bit of humor.)

Then end the spiritual exercise by opening your physical eyes.

*At first, this technique may start with the imagination, but in time Soul Travel becomes a reality.*

When you repeat this technique, Soul becomes used to going beyond the material self. At first, this technique may start with the imagination, but in time Soul Travel becomes a reality. So give it a chance. One day you'll find yourself in a higher state of consciousness, exactly as you acted it out so many times in your imagination.

Thought and imagination are powerful allies.

## Imagination Gone Wrong

The human consciousness is under the hand of the Kal, the negative power. It is a state of poor survival factors. But some people are even worse off than the general lot and bump into bad luck more often than seems their due. Why?

Mainly, it's from negative expectations. Each is a self-fulfilling prophecy, a walking disaster. You want to steer clear of such a one.

An example is the story of a young nurse. She faced a promising career at a hospital but was devastated to be fired for the habit of arriving at work late. Within a month or so, however, she found a new position. All seemed well at first.

It turned out to be a dreadful place to work. Other nurses took a strong dislike to her and used underhanded tricks to try to drive her out. Still, she hung on. But every day was a living hell. What had she done to deserve such raw treatment?

In fact, it was old karma burning off in preparation for her introduction to the teachings of ECK.

The conditions became worse. She further added to the problem by letting her imagination look for an easy way out. She begged God for deliverance from earth. She wanted to die.

How much more negative is it possible to get?

However, God turned a deaf ear to her prayers.

She raised the ante. The next prayer said this: "Please, God, make me average." Perhaps the other nurses had turned up their noses at her because she was a nurse with superior habits and skills.

Nothing in her power would melt their wall of ice.

*Thought and imagination are powerful allies.*

Her next step was to seek counseling. For a while, it looked as if the sessions might offer a hope of brighter things to come, but they never came. Stepping back, she saw that the counseling was running in circles. So she quit it. With no idea of a next best step, she nonetheless knew it was time to take charge of her own life.

The question was *how*.

Yet the decision to end counseling was a moment of truth. It changed her take on life from a negative accent to a positive one. Something would turn up. She just knew.

*A short while later, the teachings of ECK appeared in her life. She was quick to recognize the truth in them, because they held out the understanding she had sought for so long.*

Then, through a series of odd consequences, she made new patterns of thought via self-help groups, books, and the like. A short while later, the teachings of ECK appeared in her life. She was quick to recognize the truth in them, because they held out the understanding she had sought for so long. There was indeed a pot of gold at the end of the rainbow.

About the same time, an inner experience from childhood made its reappearance, and it compelled her to take steps in a new, untried direction.

But notice how her new positive expectations turned things sunny-side up.

A doctor soon offered her a job on his staff. It was a dream position, in marked contrast to the past year and a half of misery. Yet old negative thoughts died hard. At one point, she had it in mind that her death would occur a few months down the road. Her husband used every means to explain that she was only seeing the demise of her old negative state of expectations. No physical death was in her cards.

And it turned out according to his positive expectations. She lives who once was dead in spirit.

Life's been no rose garden since the day she signed up for membership in ECK, but at least she now sees the reasons for and the spiritual benefits of her trials. Pain and heartache do cleanse Soul.

The name of the next spiritual exercise is the Imaginative technique. It'll help you develop positive expectations.

### IMAGINATIVE TECHNIQUE

Soul Travel may occur in two general ways.

One form is the apparent movement of the Soul body through the planes of time and space. It is not, in fact, movement; Soul already exists on all planes. The appearance of movement, or travel, is simply the fixed states and conditions of the lower worlds coming into agreement with Soul.

That's the long and short of Soul Travel.

Let's introduce you to a prime imaginative technique for Soul Travel. Imagine a scene, and you can be there in the Soul body in the wink of an eye. It may feel like a fast trip through space, and thus the idea of travel. However, Soul Travel is the process of changing the imagined setting around you to agree with spiritual reality.

To do this imaginative technique, take a scene from your storehouse of memories and try to change some activity in it. For example, imagine the sea lashing a beach. Now imagine the turbulent waters turning still, like water in a glass. Try this technique on other mental pictures. Change a grazing horse into a running horse, and so on.

When you do this technique, you may sometime notice the faint sensation of a rushing

*The next spiritual exercise is the Imaginative technique. It'll help you develop positive expectations.*

> sound, like wind whistling in a tunnel. Again, there may be that sensation of fast movement.
>
> However, all is as it should be.
>
> Continue with the imaginative experiment, and sooner or later you'll find yourself in the mental picture of your creation, or in some other new one.
>
> Have fun with this spiritual experiment.

A second form of Soul Travel mentioned at the beginning of this section is the expansion of consciousness. This form is the true state of revelation or enlightenment that one looks for in ECK. It is a natural offshoot of the Imaginative technique.

The Imaginative technique offers a deeper insight into the ways of the ECK (Holy Spirit) and into the means of gaining love, wisdom, and freedom for yourself.

*An individual who starts the Spiritual Exercises of ECK may wonder, What is success?*

## What Is Spiritual Success?

An individual who starts the Spiritual Exercises of ECK may wonder, *What is success?* The answer could be within arm's reach.

Success is one's first meeting with the Mahanta, the Living ECK Master—the Inner and Outer Master.

"The ECKist must always practice the Kundun, the presence, whether or not he can see this inner body of the Master," says *The Shariyat-Ki-Sugmad,* Book One. "It can, however, be noted many times by the outer manifestations of things such as the protection gained, the great feeling of love which surrounds the chela, the improvement of his welfare, and the attainment of spiritual knowledge. All is given freely to the ECKist after he has passed into the higher worlds via Soul Travel."

A few years ago, an ECKist met the Mahanta right before awakening one morning. The Master handed him something. That was it. No more.

But at the ECK Worldwide Seminar that year, the Master appeared to him a second time, in a column of Blue Light. "I will walk every step with you," he said.

Then began an ordeal. The ECKist was diagnosed with cancer. As promised, the Mahanta was beside him, to give comfort, aid, and guidance every step of the way through months of treatments. Five years later, the ECKist survives.

His fears are gone. He just wants others to know the importance of always keeping love and joy for all things in their hearts.

That, too, is spiritual success.

### UNLOCKING TRUTH

The ECK always brings truth, but truth may come to each of us in different ways. The word, or mantra, you receive at an ECK initiation is your personal key to the ECK Life Stream, but you must experiment with this word.

At first you're apt to think the key is the wrong one, because it seems to open nothing. Work through this initial stage of preparation with a spiritual exercise. Use the creative technique that follows:

Chant your secret word and imagine it emblazoned upon a golden key. Fit this key into the lock of a door. Swing open the door. There, do you see? The Light and Sound of God fill the room beyond.

*The ECK always brings truth, but truth may come to each of us in different ways.*

And if that technique should run its course, try a new approach. The key is still OK, but perhaps the lock has frozen. So warm the key with a match or lighter, then insert it into the lock. It will now turn. Also experiment with lubricating oil. But whatever you do, keep working with your imagination and your personal word. Then watch! The Mahanta will feed you new ideas to try.

These exercises develop your creative powers.

In any case, a new spiritual experience of some sort will always turn up. There is always a way. This principle will stand you in good stead with any stalemate. So always look for a way out.

And be assured that your spiritual unfoldment is ever on track.

## Which Came First?

An old puzzler is the question Which came first, the chicken or the egg?

There's no big mystery about it. To my mind, the egg came first. The parents of the first chick were not quite chickens, but close. This one egg in the nest had a *mutant* chick inside. In time, some of those mutant genes mixed with those of other not-quite-a-chicken-yet fowl, and thus evolved today's chicken.

Likewise, which comes first, dream travel or Soul Travel?

There's no pat answer.

*LM tells of an occasion when Soul Travel was the first half of a two-part experience that later continued in the dream state.*

LM of Las Vegas, Nevada, tells of an occasion when Soul Travel was the first half of a two-part experience that later continued in the dream state. And then, the dream trailed over to the following night.

One morning as she did her spiritual exercise in bed, Soul Travel whisked her to a beach to meet the ECK Masters Rebazar Tarzs and Wah Z (my spiritual name). She'd been having a problem with a mental barrier. It made the path of ECK more difficult, because it had drawn her to the power of the mind instead of love. All attempts to control or overcome the mind had failed.

Love, a lesson she was to learn from the Masters, takes little effort in comparison to the energy used in a power field. Love dances, while the mind plods in heavy boots.

LM asked Wah Z and Rebazar's advice on how to be free of her rigid mind.

"My mind is holding on to old ideas and thoughts," she said. "I let them go, surrender to the ECK, and soon they return again, pestering me."

The three continued along the edge of the water. Soon the force field of an invisible barrier blocked their way. It was an absolute bar to further progress. She likened the barrier to an enormous sheet of plastic wrapping. First, tapping her creative powers to find a way past it, she charged at it, to break through. But the barrier held. Like a spring, it shot her backward through the air at a tremendous speed.

Next, LM thought of using an ordinary pin. One appeared in her hand, so she pricked the sheet; and the whole barrier collapsed. Now the path was clear. They could resume their walk.

During this test, the two Masters had kept in the background as watchers. She handled the impasse herself.

The three thus continued along the beach.

Now there came a zone of dense white mist, which she later determined was a screen of sorts

*Love, a lesson she was to learn from the Masters, takes little effort in comparison to the energy used in a power field. Love dances, while the mind plods in heavy boots.*

to guard the approach to the Etheric Plane. This plane is at the top of the Mental world.

So with no anchor points from which to tell direction in the white mist, she faced a whiteout. Uncertain of the right way to proceed, LM nevertheless hurried on. The two ECK Masters stayed close to offer aid and protection if needed. As she entered the mist, she hit a second barrier. This time, of course, the pin failed. There's no way to prick a mist and deflate it.

But she thought of something else.

The word *Baju* came to mind, and she knew it to be a charged spiritual word that allows entrance to the Etheric world. She spoke it; the mist cleared. So the small party advanced. Ahead, there appeared a round temple where the ECK Master Lai Tsi taught. The venerable Master came out to greet them. (Lai Tsi had once lived and served the Sugmad in ancient China.)

He guided LM to a room where about ten other students were seated.

Lai Tsi said, "You've all been called here to work on a specific problem. You can go anywhere on this plane to solve it."

Then he turned to LM.

"You can come here as often as it is necessary to get control over the mind."

*   *   *

The morning she sat down to write about this experience in her initiate report to the Mahanta, the Living ECK Master, she'd picked up *The Shariyat-Ki-Sugmad,* Book One. Flipping the pages at random, she stopped at a certain place.

Here's the passage that met her eyes:

"Those who listen to the Mahanta and obey with love in their hearts shall find love everywhere. They

---

*The two ECK Masters stayed close to offer aid and protection if needed.*

shall receive the love of God and shall abide in the love of the Living ECK Master."

LM, thanks to the ECK Masters, had the support she needed to control her mind and free the power of love.

In the end, it hardly matters whether dream travel or Soul Travel comes first. But it is of prime importance to catch the spiritual lessons that accompany them.

Now let's go on to the next spiritual exercise.

### BEST SLEEPING TECHNIQUE FOR SOUL TRAVEL

There are three main steps to prepare yourself for Soul Travel in the dream state:

1. Arrange your schedule to get as much sleep as needed to be fresh in the morning.

2. A few minutes before bedtime, read from one of the ECK books to signal your intent to pursue spiritual activity during sleep. Good choices are *The Shariyat-Ki-Sugmad,* Book One or Two, or *Stranger by the River.*

3. Then contemplate upon the image of the Mahanta, the Living ECK Master. In this spiritual exercise, give an invitation to the Master like this: "I welcome you into my heart as my home. Please enter it as my guest."

Then go to sleep as usual, but leave the eye of Soul (located a bit above and between the eyebrows) alert to the coming of the teacher. Look for him, because he is always with you.

*Soul's recognition of Itself comes by daily practice of the Spiritual Exercises of ECK.*

## The Daily Routine of Spiritual Exercises

Soul's recognition of Itself comes by daily practice of the Spiritual Exercises of ECK. A true knowledge of the forces of God is in them, not in books.

Rebazar Tarzs once said, "I have never valued word-knowledge which is set down in books. This leads only to mental confusion and not to such practices as the Spiritual Exercises of ECK which bring actual realization of truth."

* * *

*One's success with Soul Travel hinges upon a daily routine.*

One's success with Soul Travel hinges upon a daily routine. Early in the morning is the best time for a spiritual exercise since the day is fresh, but your family or work schedule may dictate another hour. But do a contemplation every day, at a time convenient for you.

MJD of Texas is a willing servant of God's love to all life, both inner and outer. She says, "Use me as you will."

So it's no wonder to learn of her success with Soul Travel. In fact, the ECK Masters always come to reveal more advanced and better methods. These are the secret teachings.

She's found that doing the spiritual exercise at the same hour each morning pays off. (Writers, artists, and inventors often report the same spur to their creative efforts.) One needs to set a time and place in which the Holy Spirit may flow unhindered into an expectant heart and ready mind.

So, an example of Soul Travel from MJD is the following story.

Peddar Zaskq (Paul Twitchell's spiritual name), Rebazar Tarzs, and Wah Z came to give her tips on a new and easier way to Soul Travel. Peddar said to try breathing through a single nostril.

Here is what happened:

MJD was suddenly in the family's game room in the Soul body. The room is a choice spot to do her spiritual exercises, and there she favors her husband's recliner. In the Soul body, she tried to leave the room through a window. The exit, however, was through a wall. An instant later, though, she was back in the chair, with the three ECK Masters seated alongside.

This was certainly a low-key experience. Still, it filled her with a warm and comforting love.

\* \* \*

A note is due here. New Soul Travelers sometimes worry about getting back into the physical body. That's the easy part. Soul is like a ball at the end of a rubber band, for It snaps right back in the moment the individual loses his focus. It's easy to do. Once he's free of the body, it feels so good and natural.

"Why, there's nothing to this," he says. "I've done this lots of times before."

And just that quick, the experience is over, to his great chagrin, for he ponders all the things he would have liked to see and do.

\* \* \*

Then MJD awoke in her physical body and recorded the event. After that, she followed a practice of reading a short passage from a selected book, *The Shariyat-Ki-Sugmad.* (The words, you will find, give an added dimension to any experience.)

MJD is grateful for the love and aid of the ECK Masters. Their attention, she knows, speeds her on the passage home.

*One way to leave the body via Soul Travel is to lie down after dinner when you are drowsy.*

### FIRST LANDMARKS OF SOUL TRAVEL

One way to leave the body via Soul Travel is to lie down after dinner when you are drowsy.

Plan on a five-minute nap. Then watch the process of falling asleep. If you try the exercise with your mate, agree to meet outside the body a few moments later. Now watch. Try to catch the moment that your mate was free of the physical body in a spray of radiant light and entered the next higher spiritual zone.

Of course, you the watcher are already on the higher plane.

Everyone leaves the body upon falling asleep. It is a natural, though often unconscious activity. In Soul Travel, the main difference is that we want to reach a higher state in full awareness.

*The moment Soul leaves the human body, It may pass through a blue-grey zone right above the Physical Plane.*

The moment Soul leaves the human body, It may pass through a blue-grey zone right above the Physical Plane. It takes but a moment. This zone is one approach to the Astral Plane. The sensation of moving from the Physical to the Astral body is like a mild wind current slipping through a large iris.

The iris itself is the Spiritual Eye.

Soul thus enters this neutral zone of blue-grey tones in the Astral form, a sheath that glitters like a thousand sparkling stars.

This buffer zone is a corridor between the Physical and lower Astral Planes. It's like an underground silo for an enormous rocket and is perhaps two hundred feet in diameter and two thousand feet deep. The ceiling of this circular pocket is open to the heavens. There, you may see a brilliant canopy of white light. Again, you may see a night sky sprinkled with specks of twinkling stars, or some other scene.

Whatever scene displays in the opening of the vast ceiling, Soul rises toward it at a mighty speed, and then the real journey begins.

Most people start to recall a dream only after leaving this launching pad between the two worlds, after their arrival at some faraway destination on the Astral Plane.

## Rebazar Tarzs Helps Her Soul Travel

A mother from the Netherlands felt tired one afternoon, so she lay down for a quick nap. She felt tired, yet restless. But sleep played cat and mouse with her until a lightbulb clicked on in her mind.

So she said, "Mahanta, give me an experience."

In that instant, she felt an upward surge inside her. She rose high above her resting human self, passing ocean upon ocean in the worlds beyond. Finally, she became exhausted from trying to absorb the rapid changes around her.

Then, with no warning, fear seized her on this spiritual journey.

*Am I dying?* She wondered. *What will become of my young children?*

Despite these annoying fears, this Soul Travel experience had a beautiful side. "Too sweet to stop," she said. The assurance of the ECK Masters' promise of spiritual protection must have come into play then, because the experience picked up where it had left off.

World upon world continued to flash by. Ever higher she soared, into the very canopy of heaven, beyond the limitless blue and into an arena of breathless whiteness.

This white place was the Ocean of Love and Mercy. She'd come for a foretaste of God's home. There, she found a fountain of lights, in a circle, formed like a shrine. This round fountain of light bathed her in its glory. She felt a deep, satisfying thrill of joy.

But the next instant, her physical eyes opened to the familiar sights and sounds of her own home.

*World upon world continued to flash by. Ever higher she soared, into the very canopy of heaven.*

The grand journey was over.

Still heavy with sleep, she glanced at the clock. It said 4:45 p.m. Only a short nap?

But then something, rather someone, caught her eye—the figure of a man. It was the ECK Master Rebazar Tarzs. He had guided her on this Soul Travel adventure to let her taste of God's holy temple, her true home. Now it all came flooding back. During the experience itself, though, she had been very aware of his company. Once she'd overcome the sudden rush of fear, that is.

In Soul Travel experiences prior to this one, she says, she'd never left the house.

"Now all doubt I have about ECK is totally gone," says this enlightened mom.

Two points: first, she had but to ask the Mahanta for an experience during a nap. Second, only a pure heart, free of dross, may approach the Sugmad (God).

*Two points: first, she had but to ask the Mahanta for an experience during a nap. Second, only a pure heart, free of dross, may approach the Sugmad (God).*

### CALISTHENICS

For this technique sit on the floor. Shut your eyes and stretch out your legs in front of you. Take a deep breath. Then reach for your toes with your fingertips. Stretch only as far as you can short of straining; there is no point in overtaxing your muscles with a spiritual exercise.

At the same time chant "Sugmad" *(SOOG-mahd)*.

Sing each syllable in a long and drawn-out fashion. Leaning forward, chant the first syllable, "Sug." Then return slowly to the upright position and sing "mad."

This exercise opens the consciousness for Soul to visit the higher worlds. Do this exercise for seven repetitions, then take a short rest. End the exercise with five more repetitions.

Should a Soul Travel experience result, lie down and go with it.

And, of course, the Calisthenics technique is only for someone used to physical exercise, and with the approval of his doctor. The ECK writings have a lot of other Soul Travel exercises for those who are out of shape.

## A Reality Check

Sandy, an Australian, was listening to the ECK recording "If God Is God, Then Who Are You?" A point made on the recording was that the "flying through space" experiences were a great lark. But to what end?

What benefit would such an experience afford anyone in a spiritual sense if that was the gist of it?

The Master's talk on the recording stirred old memories. Sandy had indeed enjoyed such flying experiences. They were a pleasure. But what made them stand out was the spiritual insights they brought, not just the freedom of inner flight.

Sandy's first attempts at flying while out of the body were like those of a young chicken: clumsy and exploratory. She tried harder. Despite more effort, she traveled a shorter distance still.

The Mahanta's inner voice said, "Don't be so heavy-handed."

Following his advice, she began to lift gently upward. Soon she had the confidence to maintain the gentle attention it takes to stay aloft. Now she soared in the air. Carried away by exhilaration, she tried experiments like diving and cartwheels.

*Following his advice, she began to lift gently upward. Soon she had the confidence to maintain the gentle attention it takes to stay aloft.*

What a wonderful time!

But then came a reality check.

An inner nudge from the Mahanta broke in on her aerobatics. "It's fine to have a good time," he said. "But with it must come a duty of service." The increase of spiritual powers carries with it a responsibility to turn those skills to service for others. The whole aim of unfoldment, you see, is that one day we may become a Co-worker with God.

Sandy is grateful for all the insights won through the Spiritual Exercises of ECK.

*The Shariyat-Ki-Sugmad*, Book Two, illuminates the big picture. It says: "ECK is the Audible Life Stream, the essence of the Sugmad, the Holy Spirit, and the science of God-Realization. It grows out of the experience of Soul Travel into the state of religious awareness, which the subject gains at his own volition via the Spiritual Exercises of Eckankar."

The state of religious awareness!

That's where Sandy's reality check will lead to, in the course of joyous acts of service to others.

The two go hand in hand.

*"It's fine to have a good time," he said. "But with it must come a duty of service." The whole aim of unfoldment, you see, is that one day we may become a Co-worker with God.*

### The Blue Curtain of God

The first part of this spiritual exercise is to awaken the seeing power of Soul.

Find a time to sit or lie down for ten to twenty minutes when you will not be disturbed. Shut your eyes, but imagine a dark blue curtain on the wall before you. The first few days, expect to see only the rich blue curtain. Later, some color of the Light of God will shine from it.

The second part of this exercise is to sharpen your spiritual hearing.

While looking at the blue curtain, begin to sing the word *HU* (pronounced like the word *hue*), an old name for God that saints have praised for thousands of years. After a few minutes, sing HU within yourself, making no audible sound. Continue a few minutes, then stop.

Sit quietly. Keep gazing at the royal blue curtain before you. Listen to every sound, including those that come in from outside. Among them may be a true Sound, one from the ECK, the Holy Spirit.

One more thing: Throughout this short exercise, fill your heart with love for God.

* * *

Why pray, meditate, or contemplate? Certainly, the reason must be for something other than a materialistic gain or advantage. This thing called life is your pursuit. Each must make his own way to truth, on his own path and in his own time.

The route of this quest is both a unique and solitary one. Yet all creation awaits the awakening of each individual Soul.

So why pray, meditate, or contemplate, or turn to the practice and understanding of, say, dreams?

It is so you may flourish in Spirit. Life's richness is all around you if you would but awaken, open your Spiritual Eye. Should you wish help in this life-changing, challenging pursuit, you have but to ask. The Inner Master will come.

*This thing called life is your pursuit. Each must make his own way to truth, on his own path and in his own time. Should you wish help in this life-changing, challenging pursuit, you have but to ask. The Inner Master will come.*

Beyond past lives, dreams, and Soul Travel lie the heart and spirit of life. That something is God's love.

# By the Way

*I*n *Stranger by the River*, "Jewels of Wisdom," ECK Master Rebazar Tarzs imparts a great secret to the seeker.

"The way of love is better than wisdom and understanding," he says, "for with love you can have all."

Short and sweet.

In reading to this point you've stayed the journey. Yet the greater one is still to come. Perhaps you now see that past lives, dreams, and Soul Travel are all a major part of the spiritual journey. However, none alone is its full substance, for beyond them lie the heart and spirit of life. That something is God's love.

The principle of all existence rests upon a single truth: Soul exists because God loves It.

Stop and think. If that is true, then the created is bound to the Creator. That is the secret of life. Love is all. There is nothing else. The people, places, and things about us that we take for granted are all a manifestation of God's love.

But sorrow, deprivation, loneliness, and every other expression of a negative nature are all signs of a temporary separation from God's love.

The Spiritual Exercises of ECK will help the sincere in heart find the source of divine love. This effort of returning home must come of conscious effort. It's the reason for the Spiritual Exercises of ECK.

Other Souls have trod this timeless path to God in ages past. An untold multitude. Thousands more seek it now.

Are the ECK teachings for you? Only your heart can say.

Earth is a school. It is a place to study and learn about goodness, service, and every other supreme quality by way of the lessons of everyday life. Then your Spiritual Eye will open to the Spirit of God shining in every living thing.

Think how the history of mankind might read if more enlightened Souls were to mix among the masses who stumble about in spiritual gloom.

Yet for all that, the spiritual path of ECK is an individual quest. Each person must walk it by himself.

It comes down to free will, doesn't it?

Whether or not the hour and season are right for you to set foot to the most grand adventure in life, I am sure that the words in these pages will forever change you. You will never again be the same. Soul has heard and is yearning to go home.

To find love and spiritual freedom—that's the purpose of our incarnations.

Good dreams to you, and many happy journeys.

# About the Author

Author Harold Klemp is known as a pioneer of today's focus on "everyday spirituality." He was raised on a Wisconsin farm and attended divinity school. He also served in the US Air Force.

In 1981, after years of training, he became the spiritual leader of Eckankar, Religion of the Light and Sound of God.

His full title is Sri Harold Klemp, the Mahanta, the Living ECK Master. His mission is to help people find their way back to God in this life.

Each year, Harold Klemp speaks to thousands of seekers at Eckankar seminars. Author of more than seventy-five books, he continues to write, including many articles and spiritual-study discourses. His inspiring and practical approach to spirituality helps many thousands of people worldwide find greater freedom, wisdom, and love in their lives.

# Next Steps in Spiritual Exploration

- **Try a spiritual exercise** on a daily basis.
  Example: With eyes open or closed, take a few deep breaths to relax. Then begin to sing HU (pronounced like the word *hue*) in a long, drawn-out sound, HU-U-U-U. Take another breath, and sing HU again. Continue for up to twenty minutes. Sing HU with a feeling of love, and it will gradually open your heart to God.

- **Browse our Web site: www.Eckankar.org.**
  Watch videos; get free books, answers to FAQs, and more info.

- **Attend an Eckankar event** in your area.
  Visit "Eckankar around the World" on our Web site.

- **Read additional books** about the ECK teachings.

- **Explore an advanced spiritual study class**
  (or study privately) with the Eckankar discourses that come with membership.

## Books

If you would like to read additional books by Harold Klemp about the ECK teachings, you may find these of special interest. They are available at bookstores, from online booksellers, or directly from Eckankar.

### The Call of Soul

Harold Klemp takes you on an amazing journey into a world you may have only dared to dream of—the infinite world of God's love for you. More, he shows, through spiritual exercises, dream techniques, and Soul Travel explorations, how this love translates into every event, relationship, and moment of your life. Includes a CD with dream and Soul Travel techniques.

### HU, the Most Beautiful Prayer

The simple spiritual exercises in this book will open your heart to see God's loving presence in your life. Includes a CD with the sound of thousands of people singing this powerful, majestic love song to God. Read, listen, or sing along. It lifts you spiritually, no matter your age, background, or religion.

### The Spiritual Exercises of ECK

This book is a staircase with 131 steps leading to the doorway to spiritual freedom, self-mastery, wisdom, and love. A comprehensive volume of spiritual exercises for every need.

### How to Survive Spiritually in Our Times, Mahanta Transcripts, Book 16

Discover how to reinvent yourself spiritually—to thrive in a changing world. Stories, tools, techniques, and spiritual insights to apply in your life now.

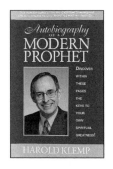

## Autobiography of a Modern Prophet

This riveting story of Harold Klemp's climb up the Mountain of God will help you discover the keys to your own spiritual greatness.

## Those Wonderful ECK Masters

Would you like to have *personal* experience with spiritual masters that people all over the world—since the beginning of time—have looked to for guidance, protection, and divine love? This book includes real-life stories and spiritual exercises to meet eleven ECK Masters.

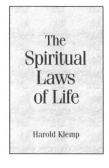

## The Spiritual Laws of Life

Learn how to keep in tune with your true spiritual nature. Spiritual laws reveal the behind-the-scenes forces at work in your daily life.

# Advanced Spiritual Study

Advanced spiritual study is available through yearly membership in Eckankar. This annual cycle of study and practice focuses on the ECK discourses, which you may study privately or in a class. Each year the spiritual student decides whether to continue with his or her studies in Eckankar.

## Discourses

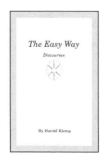

*The Easy Way*
*Discourses*

By Harold Klemp

As you explore the teachings of ECK, you will find a series of changes in your heart and mind that can make you a better, stronger, and more happy person.

Each month of the year, you'll study a new discourse and practice a new technique to enhance your spiritual journey.

The twelve lessons in *The Easy Way Discourses* by Harold Klemp include these titles and more: "In Soul You Are Free," "Dream On, Sweet Dreamer," "Reincarnation—Why You Came to Earth Again," "The Master Principle," and "The God Worlds—Where No One Has Gone Before?"

## How to Get Started

To request information about ECK books or to sign up for ECK membership and get your advanced spiritual study discourses along with other membership benefits (renewable annually), you may

- visit www.ECKBooks.org;

- join online at "Membership" at www.Eckankar.org (click on "Online Membership Application");

- call Eckankar (952) 380-2222 to apply; or

- write to:
  ECKANKAR, Att: Information, BK44
  PO Box 2000
  Chanhassen, MN 55317-2000 USA.

# Glossary

Words set in SMALL CAPS are defined elsewhere in this glossary.

**Arahata.** *ah-rah-HAH-tah* An experienced and qualified teacher of ECKANKAR classes.

**Blue Light.** How the MAHANTA often appears in the inner worlds to the CHELA or seeker.

**chela.** *CHEE-lah* A spiritual student. Often refers to a member of ECKANKAR.

**ECK.** *EHK* The Life Force, the Holy Spirit, or Audible Life Current which sustains all life.

**Eckankar.** *EHK-ahn-kahr* Religion of the Light and Sound of God. Also known as the Ancient Science of SOUL TRAVEL. A truly spiritual religion for the individual in modern times. The teachings provide a framework for anyone to explore their own spiritual experiences. Established by PAUL TWITCHELL, the modern-day founder, in 1965. The word means Co-worker with God.

**ECK Masters.** Spiritual Masters who can assist and protect people in their spiritual studies and travels. The ECK Masters are from a long line of God-Realized SOULS who know the responsibility that goes with spiritual freedom.

**Fubbi Quantz.** *FOO-bee KWAHNTS* The guardian of the SHARIYAT-KI-SUGMAD at the Katsupari Monastery in northern Tibet. He was the MAHANTA, the LIVING ECK MASTER during the time of Buddha, about 500 BC.

**God-Realization.** The state of God Consciousness. Complete and conscious awareness of God.

**Gopal Das.** *GOH-pahl DAHS* The guardian of the SHARIYAT-KI-SUGMAD at the Temple of Askleposis on the Astral PLANE. He was the MAHANTA, the LIVING ECK MASTER in Egypt, about 3000 BC.

247

**HU.** *HYOO*   The most ancient, secret name for God. The singing of the word *HU* is considered a love song to God. It can be sung aloud or silently to oneself.

**initiation.**   Earned by a member of ECKANKAR through spiritual unfoldment and service to God. The initiation is a private ceremony in which the individual is linked to the Sound and Light of God.

**Kal Niranjan.** *KAL nee-RAHN-jahn*   The Kal; the negative power, also known as Satan or the devil.

**Karma, Law of.**   The Law of Cause and Effect, action and reaction, justice, retribution, and reward, which applies to the lower or psychic worlds: the Physical, Astral, Causal, Mental, and Etheric PLANES.

**Klemp, Harold.**   The present MAHANTA, the LIVING ECK MASTER. SRI Harold Klemp became the Mahanta, the Living ECK Master in 1981. His spiritual name is WAH Z.

**Lai Tsi.** *lie TSEE*   An ancient Chinese ECK MASTER.

**Living ECK Master.**   The title of the spiritual leader of ECKANKAR. His duty is to lead SOUL back to God. The Living ECK Master can assist spiritual students physically as the Outer Master, in the dream state as the Dream Master, and in the spiritual worlds as the Inner Master. SRI HAROLD KLEMP became the MAHANTA, the Living ECK Master in 1981.

**Mahanta.** *mah-HAHN-tah*   A title to describe the highest state of God Consciousness on earth, often embodied in the LIVING ECK MASTER. He is the Living Word. An expression of the Spirit of God that is always with you. Sometimes seen as a BLUE LIGHT or Blue Star or in the form of the Mahanta, the Living ECK Master.

**Peddar Zaskq.** *PEH-dahr ZASK*   The spiritual name for PAUL TWITCHELL, the modern-day founder of ECKANKAR and the MAHANTA, the LIVING ECK MASTER from 1965 to 1971.

**planes.**   The levels of existence, such as the Physical, Astral, Causal, Mental, Etheric, and SOUL Planes.

**Rebazar Tarzs.** *REE-bah-zahr TAHRZ*   A Tibetan ECK MASTER known as the Torchbearer of ECKANKAR in the lower worlds.

**Satsang.** *SAHT-sahng*   A class in which students of ECK study a monthly lesson from ECKANKAR.

**Self-Realization.**  Soul recognition. The entering of Soul into the Soul Plane and there beholding Itself as pure Spirit. A state of seeing, knowing, and being.

**Shariyat-Ki-Sugmad.**  *SHAH-ree-aht-kee-SOOG-mahd*  The sacred scriptures of Eckankar. The scriptures are comprised of about twelve volumes in the spiritual worlds. The first two were transcribed from the inner planes by Paul Twitchell, modern-day founder of Eckankar.

**Soul.**  The True Self. The inner, most sacred part of each person. Soul exists before birth and lives on after the death of the physical body. As a spark of God, Soul can see, know, and perceive all things. It is the creative center of Its own world.

**Soul Travel.**  The expansion of consciousness. The ability of Soul to transcend the physical body and travel into the spiritual worlds of God. Soul Travel is taught only by the Living ECK Master. It helps people unfold spiritually and can provide proof of the existence of God and life after death.

**Sound and Light of ECK.**  The Holy Spirit. The two aspects through which God appears in the lower worlds. People can experience them by looking and listening within themselves and through Soul Travel.

**Spiritual Exercises of ECK.**  The daily practice of certain techniques to get us in touch with the Light and Sound of God.

**Sri.**  *SREE*  A title of spiritual respect, similar to reverend or pastor, used for those who have attained the Kingdom of God. In Eckankar, it is reserved for the Mahanta, the Living ECK Master.

**Sugmad.**  *SOOG-mahd*  A sacred name for God. Sugmad is neither masculine nor feminine; It is the source of all life.

**Temples of Golden Wisdom.**  These Golden Wisdom Temples are spiritual temples which exist on the various planes—from the Physical to the Anami Lok; chelas of Eckankar are taken to the temples in the Soul body to be educated in the divine knowledge; the different sections of the Shariyat-Ki-Sugmad, the sacred teachings of ECK, are kept at these temples.

**Twitchell, Paul.**  An American ECK Master who brought the modern teachings of Eckankar to the world through his writings and lectures. His spiritual name is Peddar Zaskq.

**vairag.**  *vie-RAHG*  Detachment.

**Wah Z.** *WAH zee*    The spiritual name of SRI HAROLD KLEMP. It means the secret doctrine. It is his name in the spiritual worlds.

**Yaubl Sacabi.** *YEEOW-buhl sah-KAH-bee*    Guardian of the SHARIYAT-KI-SUGMAD in the spiritual city of Agam Des. He was the MAHANTA, the LIVING ECK MASTER in ancient Greece.

For more explanations of ECKANKAR terms, see *A Cosmic Sea of Words: The ECKANKAR Lexicon* by Harold Klemp.

# Index

vision(s), xii, 61, 70, 160, 176–77,
    199
  of deceased, 102–3
  example of, 198
  of the One, 126
  as pre–Soul Travel event, 197
  secrets of, 207
visualization, 116
Voice of God, xii, 109
  agreement with, 177
  as birdsong, 65
  as blessing, 110
  ECK as, 207

Wah Z, 98, 121, 212, 220, 230.
    *See also* Inner Master;
    Klemp, Harold; Living ECK
    Master; Mahanta
  chanting, 176
  meeting, 180, 227
  works in dream state, 130
wake-up call(s), 6, 7, 61
waking dreams. *See* dream(s):
    waking
wealth, 19–20, 32. *See also*
    finances; money
Wheel of the Eighty-Four. *See*
    reincarnation: wheel of
Wisconsin, 45
wisdom. *See also* world(s):
    wisdom gained in
  discrediting, 9
  gaining, 171, 224
  from the heart, 84
  key to, 44, 73
*Wizard of Oz, The,* 165, 168
word(s)
  Baju (*see* Baju)
  effect of, 188
  HU (*see* HU)
  -knowledge, 230
  Mana (*see* Mana)
  secret, 155, 225
world(s)
  Astral, 68 (*see also* Plane:
    Astral)
  dream, 107 (*see also* ECK:
    dream worlds of)

Etheric (*see* Plane: Etheric)
exploring, 79, 127–28
heavenly (*see* heaven)
inner, 68, 127 (*see also*
    plane(s): inner)
lower, 4
Mental (*see* Plane: Mental)
physical, 139 (*see also* Plane:
    Physical)
of time and space (*see* time
    and space)
travel in (*see* Soul Travel)
wisdom gained in, 206

Year of Spiritual Healing, 170